OUT OF FOCUS

OUT OF FOCUS

by Peter Gordon

WARNER/CHAPPELL PLAYS

LONDON

A Warner Music Group Company

First published in 1990
by Warner/Chappell Plays Ltd
129 Park Street, London W1Y 3FA

Revised edition first published in 1997

ISBN 0 85676 138 9

Printed by Commercial Colour Press, London E7

OUT OF FOCUS

Characters (in order of appearance)

Helen Beever
Sue Dixon
Evonne Duckworth
Kath Enfield
Bob Enfield
Leonard Trotter
Wayne Bryant
David Wright
Linda Hammond

The action takes place in a church hall annexe.

ACT ONE

Scene One: A Saturday Evening.
Scene Two: Saturday evening, four weeks later.

ACT TWO

Scene One: Monday evening, three weeks later.
Scene Two: The following Saturday evening.

Time: The Present.

To my Mother and Father

EXTRACT FROM CHURCH NEWSLETTER No. 73

Friends

Once again the time has come for me to put pen to paper for our monthly newsletter.

We have a packed programme of events for the coming month and I hope to see you all making a valueable contribution to our local community.

Apologies for the recent spate of over bookings at the hall. This was caused by administrative error which should now be resolved as I have personally resumed responsibility for booking arrangements.

Rev. D. Duckworth

DATES FOR YOUR DIARY

Tues. 4th: Don't miss this one. A talk by Mrs Partridge entitled, 101 things to do with your turkey left overs.

Mon. 10th to Sat 15th: It's panto time! "Super Cinders" written and directed by E. Duckworth. Book early to avoid disappointment as seating capacity is limited to 140 for each performance.

Wed. 19th: Monthly tea and crumpet morning. All welcome.

Fri. 28th: Open to all. an illustrated talk by L. Trotter "Toad breeding for Fun and Profit".

Appeal Funds in our church bell appeal now stands at £37.41 only £2,962.59 to go!

BROWNIE NEWS

We regret to announce the resignation of our Brownie pack leader Miss H. Beever. This has partially been caused by the previously mentioned over bonking problems and we are still hopeful that Miss Beever will reconsider her position. In the meantime, all enquiries regarding Brownie events should be directed to E. Duckworth who has temporarily assumed responsibility for the group.

Church parade: Sun 23rd. Would Brownies meet at the Church Hall at 10.30 am in order to parade to the church for the service. Service commences at 10.00 am.

E. Duckworth

L. Trotter would like to announce his availability for presentation of slide shows/talks to interested groups.

He has a fine and varied selection of material to suit all age groups and interests.

Contact L. Trotter
42 The Ramblings

Polite Notice

Would users of the hall kindly refrain from smoking. There have been several recent incidents of sickness amongst our 3 to 5 year old tuesday playgroup.

Mrs Butterfield, the group organiser, feels certain that lingering fumes are responsible.

Thank you

ACT ONE

Scene One

The scene is a room in a church hall. There is a small partitioned kitchen area from which leads a back door to waste land at the rear. There is a door from the kitchen area to the main part of the room, from which there are two other exits: one to the car park outside and the other to the changing area and main hall. These are indicated by hand-written signs. Several cardboard boxes, filled with cans of food and blankets, are stacked to one side of the room.

HELEN *is shouting out of the door to the waste land. She is middle aged, plump and is wearing the uniform of a Brownie leader. She is not the type who suffers fools, or anyone else, gladly!*

HELEN   Off you go then and remember, as many pretty little leaves as you can in thirty minutes . . . what was that Suzie dear? No, you can not borrow my watch . . . not after what happened to it last time! You'll have to get watches when you go up to the Guides you know . . . very important . . . punctuality at all times.

            (SUE *enters carrying a sports bag. She is in her late twenties and is dressed in a track suit.*)

            Ah, there you are. I was just making a point about punctuality. Still, better late than never I suppose. (*She shakes hands with* SUE.) Helen Beever.

SUE   (*slightly bewildered*) Sue Dixon.

HELEN   Welcome, Susan. Nice to have you on board along with the rest of my merry little crew. Now, the girls are just out on a "nature awareness" trek. Normally Mrs Crabtree would be here but unfortunately she's down with a little bit of tummy trouble, so your extra hands will be very useful. Do you have a car, dear?

SUE   Pardon?

HELEN   Do you have a car?

SUE   No. I came by bus actually.

HELEN   Pity, would have been useful. Still, not entirely
           your fault I suppose. No uniform?

           (*During the following conversation,* SUE *begins to
           get ready for badminton, removing jewellery and
           placing it in her bag.*)

SUE   I was only a passenger. I wasn't driving it!

HELEN   (*oblivious to* SUE'S *comment*) Mmm . . . We'll
           have to see about the uniform. Can't have you
           setting a bad example to the girls can we? I see
           you've brought some sports tackle.

SUE   Yes, it's for badminton. You see I'm meeting the . .
           .

HELEN   Only one racquet? Could cause a few problems,
           dear, with twenty three girls . Still, I suppose it's
           a start; full marks for effort. (*Thoughtfully.*)
           Perhaps we could improvise something. Have a
           think about that, dear, cheap and cheerful, that's
           all that's needed.

SUE   I'm sorry but I think we must be at cross-
           purposes. You see, I'm in the Thursday night
           badminton club.

HELEN   But you don't need your shuttlecocks and what
           have you today . . . it's Saturday!

SUE   (*getting frustrated*) I know it's Saturday. We
           arranged to meet tonight.

HELEN   Yes, but when we spoke on the phone I distinctly
           said nineteen hundred hours. That's why I was
           rather surprised at you strolling in here at
           nineteen thirty!

SUE   (*now removing her watch, she finally grasps the reason for the confusion*) But I haven't spoken . . .

HELEN   Ah . . . a watch?

SUE   Yes.

HELEN   May I have a look, dear?

            (SUE *hands her watch to* HELEN *with some uncertainty.*)

HELEN   Splendid . . . just the job. Now remember, Susan, I do like to run a tight ship, and that means everybody chipping in. Alright? Now why don't you pop the kettle on while I take this out to the girls.

            (HELEN *strides out through the kitchen.* SUE *follows her.*)

SUE   Hey, that's my . . .

HELEN   (*as she exits*) Victoria, Emma, those are nettles, we don't want those!

SUE   . . . watch.

            (SUE *is totally bemused. Eventually she goes into the kitchen and switches the kettle on.* EVONNE *enters, very warily, from the car park. She is in her late thirties, a very nervous woman who is constantly defensive. She is carrying a shopping bag filled with scripts.*)

EVONNE   (*timidly*) Hello.

SUE   (*peering from the kitchen*) Hi.

EVONNE   Hello. Thought I couldn't be the first, with the door being open. Mind you, what a relief that somebody is here. I've had this dreadful feeling all day that nobody was going to turn up. I'm Evonne.

SUE   (*shaking hands*) Sue.

EVONNE   Evonne.

SUE   I'm sure the rest of the team will be here soon. I
              was a bit early.

EVONNE   The team? Yes, the team . . . I like that. I suppose
              we will be a sort of team, won't we? All pulling
              away together as it were. Super. I've got so much
              to learn, haven't I? You see I've never done this
              sort of thing before . . . not since I was at school;
              I was a little angel when I was six.

SUE   (*bewildered*) Yes . . . I'm sure you were.

EVONNE   (*wistfully*) I wanted to be a cow but they wouldn't
              let me. Nobody wanted to be my back end you
              see. (*Brightening.*) Still, maybe one day, who
              knows.

SUE   (*humouring her*) Absolutely. I'm sure if you try
              hard enough.

EVONNE   Yes, hope springs eternal. Super. (*Worried.*) Oh
              where is everybody? Do you have the time Sue?

SUE   Yeah. (*Tries to look at her watch.*) Oh, I did have.
              It's been requisitioned by the camp commandant .
              . . Arkaila or Brown Owl, whatever she's called.

EVONNE   (*panicking*) Not Miss Beever! Where is she?

SUE   She went out to muster the troops . . . troopesses.

EVONNE   She shouldn't be here, it's not her night.
              (*Reluctantly.*) Excuse me I'd better go and have a
              word.

SUE   You'll be lucky to get one in!

              (EVONNE *exits to the waste land.* SUE *continues to
              make some coffee.* KATH *enters from the car park.
              She is well groomed, casually dressed and has a
              determined expression. She is carrying a bunch of
              car keys. She is followed closely by* BOB, *who is
              wearing slacks and a sweater and carrying a
              sports bag. He looks harassed.*)

KATH   It's no use, Bob. I'm not listening to you any
        longer. She's not going and that's an end to it.

BOB   Oh come on, Kath . . . it's a conference . . . she's
        my secretary . . .

KATH   You've never needed to take a secretary before.

BOB   I know, but that was before.

KATH   Before what?

BOB   (*struggling*) Well . . . before.

KATH   (*turning on him*) I'll tell you what it was before.
        It was before you employed "luscious Linda". She
        of the fluttering eyelashes and boobs!

BOB   She does not flutter her boobs! Well, not at me
        anyway.

KATH   Stop trying to be flippant, Bob. If it was
        anatomically possible she'd do it. That girl's a
        man-eater.

BOB   Do you reckon?

KATH   Don't get any big ideas. She's not going to have a
        nibble at you is she . . . is she?

        (SUE *enters the main room, banging a saucepan.*)

SUE   End of round one! Do you want a referee?

KATH   If he mentions that woman again he'll need more
        than a referee to save him. Are you any good at
        first aid?

BOB   Tell her, Sue, you're a secretary. You need
        secretaries at conferences don't you?

KATH   What for?

BOB   Well . . . to take notes, type speeches . . . all sorts
        of miscellaneous things.

KATH   It's the "miscellaneous" things that I object to!

BOB   (*exasperated*) Will you stop twisting everything I say. Go on, Sue, tell her.

SUE   Well, I suppose there is quite often a lot of typing and stuff like that to be done. As far as the "miscellaneous" bits go . . . they're more sort of optional really.

KATH   (*finally*) In Bob's case they're not an option at all because she is not going. End of subject.

            (BOB *turns away, temporarily defeated.*)

            Nobody here yet?

SUE   Nobody here! Only a day trip from the local funny farm! So far I've met a very large Brownie who seems to be under the impression that I'm Lady Baden Powell; and some woman who's biggest ambition in life is to be a cow!

KATH   (*incredulous*) A cow?

SUE   A cow.

KATH   Did you hear that, Bob? She could take lessons from Linda.

BOB   Ha ha. (*He starts to unfasten his bag.*)

KATH   Where's my bag?

BOB   (*quietly, with feeling*) Under your eyes.

KATH   Where? Didn't you bring it in? God, it was on the back seat. I distinctly said to you "bag, Bob".

BOB   I thought you were still talking about Linda.

KATH   Here's the key, fetch it in for me will you?

            (BOB *reluctantly takes the key and exits to the car park.*)

(*shouting*) And don't forget the alarm. (*To* SUE.)
He set it off in the middle of town the other day. I
was meeting him for lunch and I gave him the key
to drop his briefcase. Anyway, off it goes just as a
police car is passing. Of course Bob, being Bob,
panicked.

SUE   Why? It's your car.

KATH   But he's banned isn't he, after the fiasco at the
last conference he went to. He was frightened that
the police would come and check up and think he
was intending driving it.

SUE   So what happened?

KATH   Silly man ran away didn't he! Ten minutes he
reckons they were chasing him.

SUE   Oh come on. I can't believe even Bob would be
that stupid.

KATH   It's true, honestly. He finally gave them the slip
in Tesco's. I can laugh about it now but at the
time I was livid. I mean, there he was with my car
keys and he goes missing for two hours!

(SUE *looks at* KATH *in disbelief.*)

He didn't dare come out again. He just pushed a
trolley round and round, taking the skin off
everybody's ankles and piling in tons of baked
beans, burgers and broccoli!

(*A car alarm sounds from the car park.*)

Oh no, here we go again! Please don't let there be
a policeman around.

(*The alarm stops.* KATH *sighs with relief.*)

He spent over seventy pounds! You don't eat
beans do you?

SUE   I know you're always going on about Bob but I
think you're really lucky. He's great, I wish I
could meet somebody like that.

KATH   (*mellowing*) He's got his good points. I just wish
            he wouldn't sulk when he isn't getting his own
            way.

SUE   Oh, I don't know, I think he's rather sweet when
            he sulks . . . a bit like a lost puppy.

KATH   But he sulks all the time, Sue; it's a permanent
            condition.

SUE   (*tongue in cheek*) Perhaps you ought to let him get
            his own way a bit more often then.

KATH   But that's the trouble with him . . . Bob hasn't got
            an own way. He's one of life's naturally gifted
            indecision makers. He'd have made a marvellous
            candidate for a cabinet minister.

            (BOB *enters, carrying a handbag which he drops
            at* KATH'S *feet as he gives her the car keys.*)

BOB   One bag.

KATH   Thank you. Trouble with the alarm again?

BOB   (*scowling*) Bloody stupid thing. It frightens me to
            death!

KATH   Well, I did remind you. Right, I'll make a start
            putting the nets up.

BOB   (*worried*) You're not staying are you?

KATH   Why shouldn't I?

BOB   But . . . you're not in the team, you'll get bored.

KATH   Bored! Bob, I am sick to death of ferrying you
            around and then going home on my own to stare
            at the walls. You need an umpire, don't you?

BOB   Yes, but . . .

KATH   So, just be grateful. The only time you're ever
            awarded any points is when *I'm* umpiring.

SUE   I'll be with you in a minute. I'll just finish this.
            (*Indicates her coffee.*)

            (KATH *exits into the main hall, leaving* BOB
            looking dismayed.)

            I hear you're really into baked beans.

BOB   Oh, she's not been telling you about that has she?
            She promised she wouldn't tell a soul. I've never
            been so embarrassed in my life.

SUE   I thought it sounded quite exciting. What's it like
            to be a wanted man on the run from the law?

BOB   It scared me rigid! I mean, as I was running away,
            down all the alley ways, I actually started feeling
            as though I'd done something really terrible. You
            know, the same feeling you get when you're
            walking through the green channel in airport
            customs . . . guilty until proven innocent!

SUE   I thought only I got that.

BOB   Oh no, everybody gets it. (*Confidentially.*) I've
            found a way round it now though. I always go
            through the red channel and declare something. I
            mean, you don't actually have to have anything   .
            . . you just say you have . . . like an extra carton
            of cigarettes or a bottle of whisky. It's perfect.
            They're happy 'cos they get the duty and you're
            happy because you don't feel guilty.

SUE   (*incredulous*) You've really cracked it haven't
            you, Bob? It's no wonder you're a wanted man,
            with a criminal brain like that. Why don't you
            turn yourself in for heroin smuggling, then you
            could really have the last laugh on them.

BOB   (*disappointed*) I should have known you wouldn't
            understand. Kath doesn't either. She thinks I've
            flipped!

SUE   I wonder why!

BOB   (*after a pause*) I wonder if they're still looking
               for me . . . the police.

SUE   (*enjoying herself*) They're bound to be. They've
               probably got a photofit in every police station by
               now.

BOB   (*worried*) What?

SUE   I wouldn't worry though, all those photofits look
               the same . . . unshaven, bent nose, eyes too close
               together. (*She looks closely at* BOB.) Oh dear, you
               are in trouble, aren't you?

BOB   It's alright for you!

SUE   Hey, you might even get on Crime Watch. Can
               you help us find this man . . . last seen wearing a
               guilty expression and impersonating a villain!

               (BOB *looks distinctly tired at having fun poked at
               him.* HELEN *suddenly bursts in through the kitchen
               looking furious.*)

HELEN   That is all I can stand! Do you know what she's
               done to me . . . to my girls? She is impossible!

BOB   (*pleasantly*) Good evening.

               (HELEN *ignores him.*)

SUE   Who's done what?

HELEN   Her . . . (*Viciously.*) the Vicar's wife. She's
               double booked me; double booked! Here am I . . .
               here are we . . . with twenty three girls all
               expecting to camp here for the night and what has
               she done?

BOB   (*helpfully*) Double booked you?

HELEN   (*still ignoring him*) She has booked the hall
               herself . . . for her ridiculous pantomime
               rehearsals. Can you believe that?

SUE	(*finally understanding*) Everything falls into place now.
HELEN	It's intolerable . . . she's intolerable.
SUE	(*cautiously*) I'm afraid I've got some bad news for you.
HELEN	Nothing, absolutely nothing, could make things worse.
SUE	Well try this. It's not us, but you, who's stuck with the twenty three girls. The reason being that I'm here for the badminton match . . . you're treble booked.
HELEN	You're not here to help! Well why did you try to deceive me earlier? (*Not waiting for an answer, she turns on* BOB.) And who are you?
BOB	Bob.
HELEN	And you're here for this . . . this match are you?
BOB	Yes.
HELEN	Have you booked the hall through the proper channels?
BOB	Yes.
HELEN	Mmm . . . do you have any suggestions?
BOB	No . . . that's four questions gone, you've got sixteen left.
HELEN	(*firmly*) Well I'm sorry but your match is cancelled.
BOB	But it can't be!
HELEN	Yes it can. Furthermore, it is. I have just cancelled it.
SUE	Helen, you can't. We've booked it, we've got another team coming.

HELEN   I'm sorry, Susan, but my girls come first. I'm a
               personal friend of the Vicar.

BOB   Well, I'm playing badminton whether you like it
               or not.

HELEN   I see. Going over my head!

BOB   You might have to duck a bit.

HELEN   We shall see about this. I'm going to telephone
               the Vicar. It's quite obvious that I will get no
               sense out of you. (*Indicating out through the
               kitchen.*) Susan, tell the girls that I will be back
               shortly.

SUE   But I'm not . . .

               (*Before* SUE *can finish the sentence,* HELEN *has
               disappeared out through the door to the car park.*
               SUE *gives a Nazi salute in her direction then
               shrugs her shoulders and sets out through the
               kitchen into the wasteland.*)

BOB   (*giving a Brownie salute*) Dib dib dib.

SUE   Dob dob dob.

               (BOB *goes into the kitchen and starts making a
               coffee. He does not hear* LEONARD *enter from the
               car park.* LEONARD *is wearing rather baggy
               trousers and a sports jacket, over which he has a
               shabby overcoat. He wears spectacles which are
               largely held together by black insulating tape. He
               carries a rather battered suitcase which is also
               patched with insulating tape. He puts the suitcase
               on the floor and exits back to the car park.*
               EVONNE *enters the kitchen from the waste land
               and meets* BOB *in the kitchen.*)

EVONNE   (*apologetic*) Excuse me, are you Bob? Sue just
               told me about the badminton.

BOB   That's right.

EVONNE   I'm Evonne. (*Grasps* BOB'S *hand and shakes it.*)
            Super to meet you. I seem to have made a bit of a
            botch don't I? . . . with the bookings. (*Babbling
            nervously.*) I only recently took over the booking
            arrangements from Donal . . . my husband . . . the
            Vicar. Do you know the Vicar . . . my husband . .
            . Donal?

BOB   Sorry, I don't believe I know any of them.

EVONNE   (*worried*) He's going to be terribly upset when he
            finds out. I don't seem to be very good at it.
            (*Hopefully.*) I don't suppose you could leave
            could you? It would help a lot.

BOB   I'm sorry but we have a match, you see. There'll
            be a visiting team . . .

EVONNE   (*pathetic*) I don't know what to do. There's the
            badminton . . . Brownies . . . my pantomime . . .
            it's such a mix up. I'm a failure aren't I? I can't
            even manage a simple little thing like bookings.
            (*Sniffing.*) I pleaded with Donal, I did; but he
            wouldn't listen. What can I do?

BOB   Look . . . don't upset yourself. It could happen to
            anyone.

EVONNE   But it wouldn't; only to me! It wouldn't happen to
            Miss Beever. (*Suddenly suspicious.*) Where is
            she?

            (EVONNE *scurries into the main room.* BOB
            follows.)

BOB   Um, I'm not quite sure it you want to know this
            but . . . I believe she's gone to ring your husband.

EVONNE   (*panicking*) What's she going to say to him!
            (*Almost bitter.*) She's a vindictive person . . . I
            know I shouldn't say it, Donal wouldn't approve
            . . . but she is, she's vindictive. (*Breaking down.*)
            And now she's gone to ring Donal.

14   ACT ONE

BOB   (*not knowing how to handle the situation*) Look,
               calm down. (*Helpfully.*) Could I get you a glass of
               water or a Bible or something?

               (BOB *rather gingerly puts his arm round* EVONNE'S
               shoulder to comfort her. He doesn't see KATH
               enter from the main hall.)

               Things are never as bad as they seem.

KATH   They'd better not be!

BOB   (*panicking*) Ah, Kath . . . this is the husband's
               wife her Vicar's the Donal . . . the Vicar.

KATH   (*icily*) In that case I would put her down before
               you get struck by lightning . . . or by me!

EVONNE   (*composing herself*) I'm sorry, I'm alright, really
               I am. It's just that nothing seems to be going very
               well.

KATH   I don't know . . . my husband seemed to be going
               extremely well. (*She smiles sweetly at* BOB.
               LEONARD *enters from the car park, carrying a
               rather ancient slide projector.*)

LEONARD   Evening.

KATH   ⎫   Hello.
BOB   ⎬   Good evening.
EVONNE   ⎭   Evening.

LEONARD   Where would you like me to set up? I thought
               over here might be best, then I can display myself
               over there.

EVONNE   I'm sorry . . . display?

LEONARD   My slides . . . the illustrated talk you booked.

EVONNE   Are you with the Brownies?

LEONARD   No. I've never been with the Brownies.
               (*Helpfully.*) I was a cub once, but that's going
               back quite a long time.

EVONNE   No, your talk . . . is it to the Brownies?

LEONARD   No, I don't think so . . . (*He starts unfolding a
            crumpled piece of paper.*) . . . not unless they like
            trains. (*Reading.*) No it isn't, I thought not. The
            Association for the Appreciation and Renovation
            of Steam Locomotives . . . Northern Area I think,
            although I could be wrong on that one . . . it may
            be Central.

EVONNE   (*with relief*) But that's next week.

LEONARD   No, I think you'll find your wrong there. I've got
            it down as tonight. Eight thirty; illustrated talk on
            famous locomotives of the forties and fifties . . .
            seventy two slides, although I expect they'll want
            to see my others of the sixties as well . . . that's
            another twenty eight, I've brought them along on
            the off chance. Anyway, if you'll excuse me I'll
            get set up.

            (EVONNE *bursts into tears and runs into the
            changing room.* LEONARD *is slightly puzzled.*)

BOB   I'm sorry but you'll have to join the queue. We're
            running out of space.

LEONARD   (*unpacking his case*) That's alright. I've worked
            in much smaller venues than this.

BOB   But was there a badminton match, a pantomime
            and a horde of Brownies in there with you?

LEONARD   (*concerned*) My equipment won't get damaged
            will it? I've had it a long time and I like to look
            after it. I won't have it tampered with.

KATH   May I make a suggestion?

BOB   You don't usually ask permission.

KATH   If this gentleman doesn't want to be interfered
            with, perhaps you could give him a hand out to
            the car park so that he can get on his way. (*She
            smiles at* LEONARD.) Alright?

LEONARD   (*in inner turmoil*) No . . . no, I can't do it . . . I
          can't let people down. If you want to see my
          locomotives, then see my locomotives you shall,
          regardless of the risk to my equipment.

KATH   I don't think you've quite grasped the situation.
          We don't want to see your locomotives . . .
          nobody here wants to see your locomotives . . .
          your locomotives are of no interest to us.

LEONARD   But I was booked.

KATH   (*getting angry*) Not by us!

          (*There is a pause during which* LEONARD *tries to
          come to terms with the situation.*)

LEONARD   (*hurt*) You don't want my locomotives then?

BOB   (*consoling*) Afraid not . . . sorry.

LEONARD   Not forties or fifties?

KATH   Especially not forties or fifties.

LEONARD   (*hopefully*) Sixties?

KATH   No!

          (LEONARD *sadly starts packing his case.*)

KATH   (*to* BOB) Do you think he's got the picture now?

BOB   (*trying to see into the suitcase*) He's got bloody
          thousands of them by the look of it.

          (SUE *limps in from the waste land. She enters the
          main room.*)

SUE   Does anybody know anything about Brownies?

BOB   Usually girls . . . about this high . . .

KATH   And very messy. You can't move in that hall for
          bags and blankets and teddy bears!

SUE   But I thought they were supposed to be helpful . . .
            courteous at all times. I only tried to get my
            watch back off them and they started throwing
            bricks at me!

BOB   (*consoling*) Probably just playfulness . . . high
            spirits of youth!

SUE   Playful . . . do you call this playful? (*She shows
            her leg which has got a large red mark on it.*)

KATH   Careful, Sue, Bob's at a very funny age.

SUE   All men are permanently at a very funny age!

BOB   Were they whole bricks?

SUE   I don't know. Does it make any difference?

BOB   It's just that I've been after some bricks for
            building a barbecue. You wouldn't like to go and
            stand there as a target again would you?

KATH   Ignore him, Sue. He's been going to build the
            barbecue for the last five years.

BOB   There's no point rushing things. I'm just waiting
            for the ozone layer to get a bit thinner . . . we
            might get a few decent summers.

KATH   By the time you get round to building it the ozone
            layer will have disappeared. We'll all be
            barbecued!

LEONARD   Earth worms.

KATH   I beg your pardon.

LEONARD   The life cycle of the earth worm and its inter-
            relationship with the keen amateur gardener.
            Forty eight slides.

KATH   (*pleasantly*) Very nice I'm sure.

LEONARD   (*pleased*) You're in luck then. I didn't think I
            had them with me, but I find that I have. It won't

take me a minute to get set up. (*He starts unpacking again.*)

KATH   (*moving to* LEONARD) I thought I'd explained. No slides.

LEONARD   But I thought it was just the locomotives you didn't want. I've got a very wide choice for you . . . I pride myself on the diversity of my displays.

KATH   (*angry*) Would you just pack up and . . .

BOB   Alright, Kath. (*To* LEONARD.) I'm terribly sorry, but think what my wife is trying to say, in her shy retiring way, is that we don't want any kind of exhibition from you at all. Now, can I give you a hand out to your car?

LEONARD   I haven't got a car. I came on my bike.

BOB   Well, I'll give you a leg up and a push off then.

LEONARD   No, I'll have to hang on here in case they turn up. (*He sits down resolutely.*) I can't let them down.

SUE   Who?

LEONARD }   The Association for the Appreciation and
BOB   Renovation of Steam Locomotives . . .

LEONARD }   Northern area.
BOB   Central area . . . one of the two.

SUE   (*bewildered*) Why do they want to see slides about worms?

KATH   Why would anybody want to see slides about worms!

(WAYNE *enters breezily from the car park. He is in his early twenties and his whole dress and attitude are geared towards impressing people with a macho image, which he uses to try to conceal his feelings of inadequacy, particularly*

towards women. He always wears a personal
stereo which he listens to when not involved in
conversation.)

WAYNE   Hi, fans.

SUE   (*in despair*) Oh, God.

WAYNE   That's Ok Sue, just call me Wayne.

SUE   (*acidly*) Wayne or pain?

LEONARD   Excuse me, but you're not here for my slides are
           you?

WAYNE   What?

SUE   How about it, Wayne? I expect you're pretty hot
           on other primitive life forms. Are you into earth
           worms?

WAYNE   (*completely confused*) Worms? Yeah, they're like
           . . . well yeah . . . (*Waving his arms vaguely.*)
           They wiggle about and that.

KATH   Well done, Wayne. Very concise summary. Come
           on Sue . . . we'd better see if your little friend has
           slit her throat yet.

SUE   My little friend?

           (SUE *and* KATH *exit to the changing room.*)

WAYNE   (*to* BOB) She doesn't fool me you know.

BOB   Who's that?

WAYNE   Sue . . . she doesn't fool me one bit.

BOB   I hadn't realized she was trying to.

WAYNE   All this crap she keeps giving me. I know why she
           does it . . . it stands to reason. She fancies me as
           much as I fancy her. She's just trying to give me
           the big come on.

BOB   I don't suppose the thought of a big push off had
           crossed your mind at all . . . no I don't suppose it had.

WAYNE   You know the trouble with you, Bob . . . you're
             out of touch. I mean, Ok, for your age you're fine,
             but you don't understand women like I do. It's a
             gift . . . I've got it and you haven't.

BOB   I don't think Kath would want me to have it!

WAYNE   Yeah, but that's another thing isn't it . . . you and
             her! You always give in to her. You ought to
             show her who's boss . . . I would. They like it.

BOB   Kath doesn't . . . she knows who's boss and she
             intends keeping it that way. She's not a great
             believer in liberation of the weaker sex. (WAYNE
             is about to interrupt.) No, I know what you're
             going to say, but take it from me, you're wrong.
             The female of the species is definitely numero
             uno.

WAYNE   What?

BOB   Number one, Wayne.

LEONARD   Excuse me a moment but I couldn't help
             overhearing your discussion and I think I might
             be able to give you the benefit of my experience
             on this particular one. Now, take spiders for
             instance . . .

WAYNE   Spiders?

LEONARD   Yes, arachnida as we call them. Now the male of
             the species has to be very careful, or else he
             might get eaten afterwards.

WAYNE   Afterwards what?

LEONARD   (*embarrassed*) You know . . . (*Winking.*) After . . .
             it.

WAYNE   Oh, you mean after . . . (*He too is embarrassed.*)
             Yeah.

LEONARD   (*enthusiastic*) If you're lucky, I might just happen
             to have a few slides with me. Talk number

eighteen if I'm not mistaken. (*He starts rummaging through his case.*)

BOB   Excuse me, but how many of these talks have you actually got?

LEONARD   (*proudly*) Seventy two . . . three. You see there's number one, that's "The small holders guide to pig breeds of the world", then there's number two, that's . . .

BOB   Pigs of the world!

LEONARD   Oh yes. Very interesting one as a matter of fact. (*Getting into his stride.*) For example, I don't suppose you know that since the last war the number of pigs in Albania has increased dramatically, whereas there has been a large decline in the number of sheep.

BOB   (*unable to believe his ears*) No, I somehow must have missed that.

LEONARD   I thought it would surprise you. Of course, there was substantial resistance from the large Muslim population.

BOB   There would be.

LEONARD   They don't eat pigs you see.

BOB   (*joking*) I suppose they have to now . . . with there not being many sheep.

LEONARD   (*serious*) Oh, I shouldn't think so. They're very strict are the Muslims . . . I do a talk about them. Would you like me to see if I've got it?

BOB   (*hurriedly*) It's very kind but I must get changed. Some other time maybe.

             (BOB *makes for the changing room as* SUE *and* KATH *enter with* EVONNE.)

KATH   (*talking to* EVONNE) Don't worry about it, we'll sort something out . . . won't we, Bob.

BOB   Sorry, changing. (*He vanishes into the dressing room.*)

KATH   (*after him*) Thank you, Bob. Wayne, I wonder if you could do something for Evonne here. She's very upset.

WAYNE   If it's a man's job, I'm your man.

KATH   It's just that there seems to be a problem outside with a pack of young hooligans. It looks as though they've dredged up some rope from the pond. They seem to be trying to organise a hanging of some sort.

WAYNE   (*nervously*) Ah, perhaps you ought to get the police. I mean I *would* go . . .

SUE   But you're scared!

WAYNE   Me scared! Come on this is me you're talking to. I just don't want to hurt anyone, Ok?

SUE   I'd have thought even you could handle some Brownies.

WAYNE   (*relieved*) Brownies? As it's for you ladies, I'll handle it, no problem. Out there? (*He points to the waste land.*)

KATH   Out there.

WAYNE   (*striding out through the kitchen*) Ok you kids. There'll be no hangings in this town while I'm sheriff.

SUE   Creep!

EVONNE   It's Miss Beever's fault. She shouldn't go off and leave them like that. (*Worried.*) I wonder what she's said to Donal . . . I wonder what he said to her!

KATH   (*kindly*) If you're that worried about it, why don't you go and ring him . . . find out.

EVONNE   Oh, I couldn't. I daren't. He'll be busy writing his
            sermon for tomorrow. And the phone's miles
            away.

KATH   No problem. Here, use the car phone. (*She gives
            the keys to* EVONNE.) It's the blue Rover.

EVONNE   Do you think I should?

KATH   Go on, do it. Then you can stop worrying.

EVONNE   (*reluctantly*) Alright then . . . I don't know what
            he'll say. He hates being disturbed when he's
            writing his sermon . . . he likes to just settle down
            with a cup of cocoa and a digestive.

            (EVONNE *is in a terrible state of nerves and starts
            to go out through the kitchen. She realises her
            mistake and goes back across to the exit to the car
            park.*)

            (*sheepishly*) Wrong way! (*She exits.*)

KATH   I've never seen such a bag of nerves! I'm
            surprised she manages to get out of bed in the
            morning without fainting.

SUE   Do you think she'll be alright?

KATH   Well we can't do any more. I'm not going to hold
            her hand while she's ringing her husband.

            (DAVID *enters from the car park. He is in his
            thirties, is dressed in a tracksuit and carries a
            sports bag.*)

DAVID   Good evening. Is this the right place?

KATH   Pantomime, match, slide show or Brownies?

DAVID   Pardon?

KATH   Sorry. Are you here to play? (*She mimes a back
            hand.*)

DAVID   Yes. None of my lot here yet?

(*The car alarm sounds outside.*)

KATH   Oh no!

DAVID   That's not your car is it? I passed a rather furtive
            looking woman on the way in . . . I said hello and
            she ran away!

KATH   It's alright. I just didn't warn her. I'd better go
            before she has heart failure!

            (KATH *exits to the car park.*)

DAVID   (*noticing* LEONARD) Good evening.

LEONARD   How do you do.

            (BOB *rushes out of the changing room. He has no
            shoes or trousers on.*)

BOB   Kath, that's our car!

            (EVONNE *runs in and sees* BOB. *She gasps.*)

EVONNE   (*apologetically*) Sorry.

            (EVONNE *runs out again.*)

SUE   It's alright, Bob. Everything is under control.

BOB   Are you sure?

SUE   Yes. This is one of our opponents. (*She indicates*
            DAVID.)

            (*The alarm stops.*)

BOB   (*forgetting his state of undress*) Pleased to meet
            you. Bob Enfield. (*He shakes hands with* DAVID.)

DAVID   David Wright . . . police second team.

BOB   (*horrified*) Police! (*Trying to hide his face during
            the remainder of the conversation.*) Great . . . I
            suppose there's quite a few police people in your
            team then?

DAVID	That's the idea, yes. (*He notices* BOB *standing with his neck at an awkward angle.*) Are you alright?
BOB	Yes, fine. Excuse me a moment. (*He pulls* SUE *over to one side.*) Get rid of him. We'll have to cancel the match.
SUE	What for?
BOB	Police! I'm wanted aren't I?
	(DAVID *and* LEONARD *strike up a conversation.*)
DAVID	Are you here to watch?
LEONARD	No, I was rather hoping that you might be.
SUE	Oh, come on, I was only joking. I'm sure the police don't have a clue who they were chasing. They do have other things to do you know.
BOB	It's alright for you to say that. It's not your freedom that's at stake! What's he doing?
LEONARD	I don't suppose you're interested in trains are you?
DAVID	No, sorry.
LEONARD	I didn't think you looked the type. They aren't either.
	(DAVID *looks over towards* BOB *just as* BOB *is sneaking a look.*)
BOB	He's watching me!
LEONARD	They were very rude to me. I was only trying to be friendly.
DAVID	I'm sure they didn't mean it.
	(DAVID *walks over to* BOB.)
BOB	He's coming over!

DAVID   (*joking*) I've had a complaint about you.

BOB   Oh, God. (*He rushes out to the changing room.*)

DAVID   Was it something I said?

SUE   Er . . . no, I shouldn't think so . . . he's in
             training. You know what it's like, all that energy .
             . . he just suddenly rushes off somewhere. It
             happens all the time.

DAVID   Oh, right. I like to keep in shape myself. Running
             mainly . . . I do the odd marathon, you know.
             Actually, he looks familiar . . . I wonder if that's
             where I've seen him . . . does he do marathons, do
             you know?

SUE   (*trying to suppress a laugh*) Bob . . . marathons!
             Er, no I don't think so . . . I think he's more into .
             . . body building . . . it hasn't worked yet.

DAVID   Now, that's something I wouldn't mind having a
             go at. I might have a word with him.

SUE   Yes, I'm sure he'd like that.

             (*There is a mutual attraction and they smile
             stupidly at each other.*)

DAVID   How long have you been playing then?

SUE   Oh, a few years now. I'm not all that good, I just
             do it for the exercise really.

DAVID   Yeah, it's a lot more strenuous than most people
             think. It's a great game, no doubt about it . . . do
             you use pimples?

SUE   Pardon?

DAVID   Pimples, you know.

SUE   (*uncertainly*) No . . . I've always tried to avoid
             them as much as possible. It's probably Wayne
             you want to be talking to.

(HELEN *storms in from the car park. She is in a rage.*)

HELEN   Where is she?

SUE   Who?

HELEN   That viper. She's turned him against me. I never had any trouble with Donal . . . the Reverend Duckworth until she came along.

SUE   You know him well then?

HELEN   Donal? If only you knew the half of it, Susan. I used to do so much with him . . . we always got on so well. Church parade, garden parties, the annual flower show. I had hopes, Susan. I always felt that eventually . . . then *she* came along.

SUE   I gather he wasn't tremendously helpful then, on the phone?

HELEN   (*almost weeping with frustration*) The match . . . that has priority . . . then the pantomime and then my girls. All the preparation . . . (*Indicating the boxes.*) . . . the food, the organisation! It's a sorry state, Susan, a sorry state!

LEONARD   Excuse me, but he didn't happen to mention my slides did he?

HELEN   (*to* SUE) Who is that?

SUE   He's just passing through.

HELEN   (*looking at* LEONARD *suspiciously*) He's not a tramp is he?

SUE   I don't think so.

HELEN   But look at the state of him. I suppose they'll be turning this into a soup kitchen next! (*She spins round to* LEONARD.) This isn't a soup kitchen you know.

(LEONARD *looks baffled.*)

	(*turning back to* SUE) I don't know how I'm going to break this to my girls. How do you do it? How do you break the hearts of twenty three girls?
SUE	Ask Wayne. According to him it's a way of life.
HELEN	Wayne? Who's Wayne, is that you? (*Turning to* DAVID.)
DAVID	No, sorry, David Wright.
HELEN	I see. I suppose you're one of this team are you?
DAVID	Afraid so; police seconds.
HELEN	You're a policeman?
DAVID	For my sins, yes.
HELEN	(*warming to him*) Uniformed?
DAVID	Yes.
HELEN	I'm very pleased to meet you, David. (*She shakes his hand.*) Helen Beever . . . Miss . . . It's so nice to meet another member of the uniformed services. We all have to do our little bit don't we? Me with my girls and you with the rest of your boys in blue. Tell me, David, is there a Mrs Wright?
DAVID	(*smiling*) I'm sure there is but I haven't met her yet. (*He glances over at* SUE.)
HELEN	Pardon, David?
DAVID	(*explaining*) Mrs Wright . . . Mrs right.
HELEN	Oh yes, I see. Perhaps we could get together sometime for a chat. I have a tremendous feeling that we have so much in common, I really do.
DAVID	(*trying to keep a straight face*) Really?
HELEN	Oh yes, undoubtedly. I noticed a certain . . . affinity as soon as I saw you. What are your interests?

DAVID   I don't know, not too much really. Keeping fit . . .
               I used to enjoy getting involved with drama. I
               heard you talking about a pantomime just now . . .
               I'm rather tempted to have a go.

HELEN   The pantomime!

DAVID   Yes . . . obviously not one of your interests.

HELEN   What . . . me? Oh, I've been looking forward to it
               for months. I wouldn't miss it for the world . . .
               tremendous fun. (*She tries to smile
               enthusiastically but doesn't quite succeed.*)

               (BOB *enters. He is dressed for badminton but has
               a towel round his shoulders which is pulled high
               over his face.* SUE *goes to him.*)

SUE   What on earth are you doing?

BOB   Disguise, isn't it. If we can't cancel the match
               I've got to do something.

SUE   You can't wear that all night!

BOB   Like to bet? (*He waves to* DAVID.) Alright?

DAVID   Yes thanks. Fancy a quick knock up?

BOB   Yeah, great. I'll be with you in a minute. (*To
               SUE.*) See, no worries.

               (KATH *enters with* EVONNE *who is looking
               distraught.*)

KATH   Never mind, Evonne . . . I'm sure you just caught
               him at a bad time.

EVONNE   I shouldn't have rung him . . . he gets very intense
               when he's writing his sermon. I've made an awful
               mess of absolutely everything, haven't I?

HELEN   Yes.

               (EVONNE *sobs.*)

KATH   (*angrily to* HELEN) Do you mind! (*Turning to*
                EVONNE.) It's no use getting yourself upset again.
                What about this pantomime of yours? You can
                show your husband what you're really capable of.

EVONNE   I'm not capable of anything. I'm going to cancel it.

KATH   (*enthusiastically*) Nonsense, it's going to be a
                huge success. We'll help you, won't we . . . Sue,
                Bob, we'll help with the panto won't we?

BOB   (*now sorting things out in his bag*) Don't rope me
                in to it, I haven't got the time. (KATH *glares at
                him.*) I've got a barbecue to build.

KATH   (*over-ruling him*) Rubbish! It's about time you
                developed a few healthy interests . . . with *me*.
                There you are, Evonne. That's three of us already.

HELEN   And we'll help as well won't we, David?

EVONNE   (*accusingly at* HELEN) You! After all the things
                you said to Donal.

HELEN   (*for* DAVID's *benefit*) It's obviously all just been
                an absurd misunderstanding. I can't see what all
                the fuss is about, I really can't. We'd love to be
                involved wouldn't we, David?

                (DAVID *smiles at her and then goes to his bag to
                take out a table tennis bat. There is a muffled cry
                from out in the waste land.*)

                What was that?

KATH   What?

HELEN   I thought I heard something.

                (BOB *and* DAVID *meet.* BOB *has a badminton
                racquet and* DAVID *his table tennis bat.*)

BOB   Ok?

DAVID   Ready when you are.

*(They suddenly realise the problem. There is a
long pause as they look at each other.)*

BOB   This isn't going to work is it?

DAVID   But I thought . . . I'm sure it's tonight.

           *(They both start laughing. There is another
           muffled cry from outside the kitchen.)*

HELEN   There it is again!

           (WAYNE *struggles in through the kitchen. He is
           bound, hand and foot, and gagged with a
           handkerchief. He hops into the main room.)*

KATH   *(laughing)* What's happened?

           (WAYNE *hops over to* KATH *and she starts to undo
           the gag.)*

SUE   No, leave it. He's much better like that.

DAVID   *(to* BOB) Have you got a cold or something?

WAYNE   *(gasping for air)* They're mad . . . lunatics!

HELEN   You haven't been harming my girls . . . I know all
           about men like you!

WAYNE   Me . . . harm them! They said it was just a game
           practising their knots!

SUE   Into bondage are you?

WAYNE   Then they turned vicious . . . they were going to
           drown me!

SUE   And you've spoilt their fun?

           (LINDA *enters from the car park. She is attractive
           and is dressed "to be noticed".* BOB *sees her and
           tries to hide his face even deeper in the towel.)*

LINDA   Excuse me, is this the right place?

KATH   *(turning)* It depends what you're after . . . *(She
           suddenly recognises her.)* . . . I know what you're
           after!

LINDA   I'm sorry, I don't . . . (*Horrified.*) You're Kath!

KATH   (*marching over to* BOB *and pulling the towel off
             him*) Look, Bob . . . what a nice surprise, Linda's
             here to see you!

BOB   (*feigning surprise*) Linda, what are you doing
             here?

KATH   (*angrily*) I've think you've got some explaining,
             Bob!

WAYNE   Hey, what about me? Get this stuff off me
             somebody.

SUE   (*to* WAYNE) Oh, shut up, Wayne.

             (SUE *gives* WAYNE *a push and he topples over
             backwards.*)

DAVID   (*to* BOB) I'm sure I know you from somewhere.

KATH   Well, Bob. What have you got to say?

LINDA   (*to* LEONARD) I seem to have come at rather a bad
             time!

LEONARD   (*hopefully*) Do you like steam engines?

             (*Curtain falls.*)

Scene Two

A rehearsal night four weeks later. BOB *and* SUE *are sitting
together,* BOB *looking through his script and* SUE *sewing one
of the costumes.* DAVID *and* LEONARD *are busy working on
scenery.* DAVID *is painting a "stand up flat" of a stove with a
saucepan on it.* LEONARD *is working next to* DAVID *on his own
special project which, though in its early stages, is a large
flat, shaped as a coach. It has a cut out window so that the
person carrying the coach appears to be travelling in it.
Several other half finished props and pieces of scenery are
scattered around the room. As the curtain opens,* LEONARD *is
just unpacking some dubious looking sandwiches from his back
pocket.*

BOB	God, this is impossible!
SUE	What is?
BOB	Trying to learn this lot. It wouldn't be so bad if it made any sense.
LEONARD	Sandwich anybody?

(*They all look at his sandwiches and politely decline.*)

BOB	No thanks, Leonard . . . I'm on a diet.
DAVID	I thought you were in to body building?

(BOB *looks puzzled.*)

SUE	(*hurriedly*) I mentioned it, Bob . . . on that first night.
BOB	Oh . . . no, Kath made me give up when my thighs got as big as hers.
LEONARD	I like well-built women.
BOB	(*joking*) Have you got any slides . . . (*Touching his nose.*) . . . know what I mean?
LEONARD	(*serious*) Sorry, I haven't no.

(*They return to their various tasks and* LEONARD *munches a sandwich.*)

(*to* DAVID) Do you enjoy being the cat then?

DAVID	I was hoping for something a bit more substantial. I'm the only one of us who's done any drama before . . . and who does Evonne cast me as?
LEONARD	They're fascinating animals actually . . . felis catus as I like to say. Perhaps I could give you a few tips for your characterisation.
SUE	(*to* BOB) Kath talking to you yet?

BOB	Fat chance! That's four weeks now. All I've heard her say is "you're a very wicked person".
SUE	It's a start I suppose.
BOB	No . . . it's one of her lines from the panto. She just seems to be practising that particular one every time she walks past me.
SUE	Well, you'll have to start talking again sometime.
BOB	I've tried. I told her that Linda just turned up out of the blue for the auditions . . . that it was nothing to do with me.
SUE	So, why won't she believe you?
BOB	(*guilty*) 'Cos it's not true . . . I probably don't sound very convincing. I'm not very good at acting.
SUE	Yes I'd noticed. You knew Linda was coming then?
BOB	I didn't think Kath was staying that night. I told Linda to come along so that I could show her how to play.
SUE	(*accusingly*) Play what?
	(EVONNE *pokes her head round the corner from the main hall.*)
EVONNE	(*cheerfully*) Could I have the Baron and Prince Charming please . . . super.
SUE	Coming.
EVONNE	Super.
SUE	(*scolding* BOB) I'm not surprised Kath doesn't talk to you. (*Rising and speaking to* LEONARD.) Come on, Baron.
LEONARD	Pardon?
SUE	We're wanted.

LEONARD	Right you are. Just hang on a second . . . this is quite a tricky bit. (*He works intensely on the coach for several seconds.*) There that's got her. (*As he exits with* SUE.) I was just telling David about cats. I thought it might help him get it across.
	(SUE *ushers* LEONARD *out to the main hall. As she exits she gives* DAVID *a wave.*)
DAVID	I know he means well but I wish he knew when to shut up.
BOB	(*moving over to* DAVID) My condolences. He does seem to have taken you under his wing a bit.
DAVID	Well, it's not so bad I suppose. It's Helen who's causing the problems at the moment. She still seems to be under the impression that romance is just around the corner. I don't know what to do to shake her off.
BOB	I don't think I'm the right person to talk to about personal relationships.
DAVID	I'm not trying to get into one, I'm trying to avoid one. How do you tell someone nicely that you're not interested.
BOB	I just act myself. Eventually they tell me *they're* not interested.
	(HELEN *and* LINDA *enter from the main hall.* HELEN *is complaining to* LINDA.)
HELEN	I can not tolerate that woman one moment longer. Have you seen the way she deliberately sets out to humiliate me? It's obvious that I am far more accomplished in the subtleties of the theatre than her. (*She spots* DAVID *and her nature instantly changes.*) Why, David, how nice to see you . . . and how is my favourite little pussy cat?
DAVID	(*cringing*) Fine thank you, Helen . . . fine.

BOB   Something upset you has it?

HELEN   Her! Trying to make me a laughing stock. I had
               reservations from the very first day when she cast
               me as an ugly sister.

BOB   Type cast again, eh?

HELEN   And I will thank you, Bob, to keep cheap jibes to
               yourself.

BOB   I'm an ugly sister as well you know.

HELEN   Yes, but it suits you. Now then, David, have you
               been out and about today in that smart little panda
               car of yours? You must tell me all about it.

               (HELEN *ushers* DAVID *over to two chairs. He looks
               pleadingly at* BOB. *Enjoying* DAVID'S *predicament,*
               BOB *walks away singing the opening bars from
               "Some Enchanted Evening". He sits down and
               opens his script but his enjoyment is short lived
               as* LINDA *comes over and sits beside him.*)

LINDA   Hi, Bob.

BOB   (*horrified*) You're not sitting there are you?

LINDA   (*smiling*) I seem to be!

BOB   (*panicking*) But you can't! What if Kath comes
               back and sees us? Can't you sit over there
               somewhere?

LINDA   How can we have a cozy chat if I'm over there?
               You're a big boy now. Kath does allow you to
               talk to people doesn't she?

BOB   Yes, but she's rather selective. You're on the
               blacklist at the moment!

LINDA   And you follow orders do you? Are you a man or
               a mouse?

BOB   *(having to think about it)* A man of course . . . it's
           just that when Kath gives me one of her looks I
           tend to develop a slight squeak!

LINDA   *(scathing)* And run off to hide in your little mouse
           hole. Does she know I'm going with you to the
           conference next week?

BOB   I did try to discuss it with her a few days ago.

LINDA   And?

BOB   She didn't seem keen.

LINDA   But what happened?

BOB   Well . . . I rang her up and said . . .

LINDA   Rang her up!

BOB   It seemed safer . . . she can get very physical
           sometimes. I rang her up and tried to explain the
           situation in a mature adult way . . .

LINDA   Yes?

BOB   . . . You don't know anybody who repairs phones,
           do you?

LINDA   *(exasperated)* Does she know I'm going?

BOB   I'm not sure, but I think I may have left her with
           the impression that you're not.

LINDA   Squeak squeak.

BOB   Squeaking and running away is better than getting
           your bloody neck broken in the trap!

LINDA   It sounds to me as though you're already in the
           trap.

BOB   *(sadly)* Maybe you're right. The thing is, I think I
           like the cheese.

LINDA   What?

BOB   It doesn't matter.

LINDA	I want to go to this conference, Bob. We could have a great time. Don't you want me there?
BOB	Of course I do . . . it's just Kath.
LINDA	So am I going or not? Most men would jump at the chance.
BOB	I know . . . just don't hassle me. I'll sort it out.

(SUE *and* WAYNE *enter from the main hall. They are talking to each other.*)

WAYNE	Of course, I find it easy. I mean I could have easily taken it up proficiently . . . proffisionitly . . . as a job. People thought I could have been the next Schwartzer . . . Shwatser . . . Shutser . . . Tom Hanks
SUE	(*bored*) Been to RADA have you?
WAYNE	(*lost*) Where's that . . . Portugal is it?
SUE	Oh come on, Wayne . . . South America.
WAYNE	Oh yeah . . . near Portugal.
SUE	I'm going to make the coffee. (*She goes into the kitchen.*)
WAYNE	Strong and black for me . . . like my women!
LINDA	(*to* BOB) I bet he wouldn't say no to a weekend away with me.
BOB	I don't think Wayne would say no to a weekend away with a dead whelk.
LINDA	(*angry*) Fine! So that's what you think of me is it?
BOB	You know I didn't mean it like that.
SUE	(*calling*) Everyone for coffee?

(*They all call "yes please", etc.*)

DAVID	(*trying to escape from* HELEN) I'll give you a hand.

HELEN   And me.

DAVID   No, it's alright, Helen. You stay there and take it easy for a while.

          (DAVID *goes into the kitchen.*)

SUE   (*aware of his attempt to escape*) Any port in a storm?

DAVID   (*smiling*) She certainly puts the wind up me!

LINDA   (*to* BOB) We'll see who the real man is.

          (LINDA *stands and goes towards* WAYNE.)

BOB   (*calling after her*) You'll never get rid of him.

LINDA   (*turning back to* BOB) Maybe I won't want to! (*She goes up to* WAYNE.) Hello, Wayne.

WAYNE   Oh, hi, Linda. How's things?

LINDA   Fine . . . I think you're doing really well in that part as Buttons.

WAYNE   Yeah, I thought so as well. I suppose I've just got a natural talent for it.

LINDA   (*seductively, for* BOB's *sake, who she knows is watching*) And what other natural talents do you have, Wayne?

WAYNE   Oh, I don't know. I'm a bit of an all rounder . . . pretty good at most things. I keep it to myself though . . . I don't like bragging about it.

LINDA   (*cringing*) So modest as well.

WAYNE   Yeah, well I have to be. I can't give too much away . . . it's my job you see.

LINDA   What is that . . . what do you do?

WAYNE   Sorry, Linda, I'm not allowed to say. (*Confidentially.*) It could put us both in danger if it got out . . . know what I mean?

LINDA	(*playing along with him*) So mysterious! go on Wayne, I won't tell a soul . . . cross my heart.
WAYNE	Hey, I'd like to but . . . Ok, this is just between you and me. (*He checks that nobody is listening.*) You heard of the SAS?
LINDA	(*feigning amazement*) Yes?
WAYNE	That's me.
LINDA	(*trying not to laugh*) Just you?
WAYNE	Well, no . . . there's a few of us. Special Air . . . (*Hopefully.*) Squadron.
LINDA	I always thought it was Service!
WAYNE	(*flustered*) Oh yeah . . . them. They're not bad . . . we're a bit more hush hush. I'm on extensive leave at the moment. (*Checking behind him again.*) My last mission was in RADA, that's South America.
LINDA	I've always wanted to meet one of you guys. You must be pretty tough.
WAYNE	(*casually*) I get by. It's the training you see . . . prepares you for anything. (DAVID *accidentally drops a tray of cups in the kitchen.*) Bloody . . . (WAYNE *jumps in surprise and accidentally bangs his head on the wall. He staggers away from it clutching his head.*) . . . Christ!
DAVID	Sorry.
LINDA	(*suppressing giggles*) Are you alright, Wayne?
WAYNE	(*trying to shrug it off*) Yeah, fine . . . no problem . . . sorry 'bout that . . . it's the training. Reaction stuff, you know . . . react first then think.
LINDA	You're great at the first bit.

WAYNE   Yeah, right . . . (*Still holding his head and
            staggering slightly.*) Mind if we sit down a
            minute?

            (*They sit down together.* WAYNE *is still rather
            groggy.*)

DAVID   (*to* SUE) I don't know what happened, it just
            slipped through my fingers.

SUE   Don't worry . . . most of them bounced.

DAVID   I'm surprised you got yourself involved in all this
            panto business.

SUE   Am I that bad?

DAVID   No . . . I didn't mean that. You're good. I just
            meant that I thought you'd be too busy with other
            things.

SUE   I didn't actually have a lot of choice . . . I got
            volunteered. Anyway what else should I be doing?

DAVID   I don't know. You must have lots of boyfriends.

SUE   I've given them up.

DAVID   That's a pity . . . for the boys.

SUE   I'm sure they'll survive. Anyway, what about you?

DAVID   No, I've given them up as well. (*Looking out at*
            WAYNE *and* LINDA.) I see Wayne's trying his hand.

SUE   I don't think she's likely to bite it off! Mind you,
            if she started she'd probably swallow him whole!

DAVID   Yes, I know what you mean. Bob looks a bit
            chewed up.

            (*They look over at* BOB *who is sat watching* LINDA
            and WAYNE.)

SUE   Serves him right. He deserves anything he gets. In
            a way I hope Wayne has a bit more success.

DAVID   I thought you couldn't stand him!

SUE   I can't. It's just that then she'd keep away from
             Bob.

DAVID   Maybe I ought to get him to chat Helen up.

SUE   You should get out of it so easily! Anyway,
             Wayne's alright. I just can't stand his constant
             idiotic prattle. It's like his brain's living on
             another planet.

DAVID   Probably just insecure.

SUE   Yeah. He still lives with his Mum, you know . . .
             just the two of them. He's not half as tough as he
             likes people to think.

WAYNE   (*to* LINDA) Course I'm a lot tougher than people
             think. I have to play it down.

LINDA   (*seeing* BOB *watching them and taking* WAYNE'S
             hand) How about telling me more about it later?

WAYNE   (*looking around, rather embarrassed*) Sure . . .
             (*He takes his hand away.*) . . . after coffee?

LINDA   I was thinking of much later than that. How about
             taking me out after we're finished here?

WAYNE   (*not believing what he's heard*) What . . . you
             mean you and me and you!

LINDA   Don't you want to?

WAYNE   . . . No it's not that . . . great, Ok . . . but we
             won't be finished here 'til gone nine!

LINDA   Not frightened of the dark are you?

WAYNE   What, me? No, great . . . it's just that when I have
             a night out I usually start really early. You know,
             when I go out with the lads we're pretty crazy
             guys, yeah?

LINDA   (*smiling seductively*) But it's not the lads is it?
             Just you and me.

WAYNE   . . . Yeah . . . right.

SUE   (*calling out*) Coffee everyone.

             (LINDA *looks to see whether* BOB *is watching. He
             is, so she blows* WAYNE *a kiss as she moves
             away.*)

LINDA   See you later then.

             (SUE *goes to call out through into the main hall.*
             LINDA *goes to get her coffee from the kitchen
             counter.*)

SUE   (*calling into the main hall*) Coffee up, Evonne.

             (SUE *returns to the kitchen.*)

HELEN   Just one sugar for me, David. Must keep in shape.

SUE   (*to* DAVID) I wouldn't have thought she'd want to
             stay that particular shape! (*Calling to* HELEN.)
             Actually it's self service, Helen.

HELEN   Yes I know, dear, but I'm sure David won't mind.

DAVID   (*resigned*) Coming up.

             (DAVID *takes a coffee to* HELEN *as* BOB *goes over
             to get his.*)

BOB   (*to* DAVID) It's alright waiter, I can manage my
             own!

             (WAYNE *is standing to one side looking rather
             anxious as he counts his money and searches his
             pockets for more.* HELEN *is about to engage* DAVID
             in conversation when she is interrupted by WAYNE
             calling to DAVID.)

WAYNE   'Scuse me, David. Got a minute?

DAVID   (*thankfully moving from* HELEN) Yeah?

WAYNE   I was wondering if you'd do me a bit of a favour.

DAVID   Like what?

WAYNE   Well normally I'm pretty flush . . . you know,
               never less than a couple of hundred on me.
               Trouble is something's come up and I've left my
               wallet at home. I was wondering?

DAVID   I'm sorry, Wayne but . . .

WAYNE   I'd pay you back tomorrow . . . (*Hopefully.*) . . .
               or next week if that would suit you better.

DAVID   Ok, but as I was saying I've hardly got anything
               on me. I meant to call at the cash point. I've got a
               couple of pounds if that's any help.

WAYNE   Oh yeah, that'd be great. (*Casually.*) It's to take
               Linda out actually . . . thought I'd show her a
               good time.

DAVID   Linda! Good for you. Don't you think you might
               need a bit more?

WAYNE   No problem. I've got a bit on me already, it's just
               to make sure really.

DAVID   (*handing over two pounds*) Don't spend it all at
               once!

WAYNE   Great, thanks. (*Counting his money.*) That's . . .
               just over four pounds.

DAVID   Four pounds! You really are going to have a wild
               time aren't you!

               (WAYNE *counts his money again, looking very
               worried.* DAVID *resumes his painting, avoiding*
               HELEN *who is trying to attract his attention.*
               EVONNE, KATH *and* LEONARD *enter and go to
               collect their coffee.*)

EVONNE   I think rehearsals are going absolutely splendidly.
               Don't you think so?

               (*Everyone remains quiet.*)

Super! . . . What do you think Mr Trotter?

LEONARD   Well, in my experience, I think you'll find that it
           will get better as time goes by . . . once you've
           got the hang of what you're doing.

EVONNE   (*horrified*) But I thought I had!

LEONARD   No, but what I meant by that was that it takes a
           bit of time to get into it . . . get you're directions
           right and so forth. At the moment you're more
           "on your learning curve" as I like to call it.

EVONNE   Kath?

KATH   (*trying to sound confident*) Nothing to worry
           about, Evonne. A bit of perseverance and I'm sure
           it won't be lacking. It'll be . . . wonderful.

EVONNE   You think it's awful don't you? You all do!

KATH   No . . . good heavens no. It's . . . developing.

LEONARD   (*helpfully*) If it doesn't quite get off the ground I
           don't mind standing in with a talk.

EVONNE   (*very upset*) I knew it . . . I just knew it!

           (EVONNE *flees to the changing room.*)

KATH   (*to* LEONARD) I don't think that was quite what she
           wanted to hear!

           (LEONARD *moves to talk to* DAVID, *who visibly
           cringes as he approaches.* KATH *goes over to*
           BOB.)

           Had a cozy time in here with Linda have we?

BOB   We said hello . . . it's alright for us to say hello
           isn't it?

KATH   No it is not.

           (KATH *storms out after* EVONNE. BOB *is looking
           totally defeated as* WAYNE *approaches him.*)

WAYNE   Excuse me, I was wondering?

BOB   (*taking his frustration out on* WAYNE) I thought
               that required a brain!

WAYNE   What?

BOB   I'm sorry, Wayne. What can I do for you?

WAYNE   You couldn't lend me a couple of pounds could
               you? I'd pay you back . . . it's just that
               something's come up.

BOB   Yes, alright. Don't leave the country. (*He gives
               two pounds to* WAYNE, *then suddenly realizes*.)
               What's it for?

WAYNE   Oh, just taking Linda out . . . I think I've scored.

BOB   In that case you can use somebody else's money!

WAYNE   What!

               (BOB *snatches the money back.* WAYNE *looks
               bewildered.* BOB *has second thoughts and hands
               the money back.*)

BOB   Oh, never mind . . . here. (*With as much good
               feeling as he can manage*.) Have a good time.

WAYNE   Great . . . thanks.

               (WAYNE *turns to walk away*.)

BOB   Just one thing, Wayne. You didn't score . . . it
               was an own goal . . . mine.

WAYNE   (*confused*) What?

BOB   (*forcing a smile*) Enjoy yourself.

               (*As* WAYNE *walks away he is intercepted by*
               LINDA.)

LINDA   Where are you taking me then?

WAYNE   Thought we could hit the Blacksmith's Arms.

LINDA	(*horrified*) The Blacksmith's Arms?
WAYNE	Yeah, it's pretty smart in there these days. It's been done up . . . you know . . . proper imitation oak beams and all that.
LINDA	But it's full of creeps!
WAYNE	I like it . . . I go there a lot.
LINDA	I thought you might want to take me somewhere a bit more exciting. There's a great new night club in town . . . couldn't we go there?
WAYNE	(*panicking*) Yeah . . . we could . . . it's just the last bus you see . . .
LINDA	But I thought you said you had a car . . . an XR something?
WAYNE	Oh yeah, the XR GTI-S Turbo . . . injection. I'm not in it tonight, it's being customised . . . new stripes, all that sort of stuff.
LINDA	Never mind . . . I can give you a lift home, it's no problem.
WAYNE	(*seeing no way out*) Right . . . great.
LINDA	That's settled then . . . meal, then a night club.
	(LINDA *saunters over to* BOB, *leaving* WAYNE *in a panic. During the following speeches,* WAYNE *desperately searches his pockets again.*)
LINDA	At least some men aren't frightened to take me out.
BOB	(*defensively*) I'm not frightened . . . just married!
LINDA	Same thing isn't it?
BOB	Of course it isn't. Being frightened is a state of mind . . . being married is a state of your partner's mind.
LINDA	Oh, very good. Turning into a philosopher now.

BOB   I've always been philosophical . . . you have to be
               when you're married to Kath!

LINDA   Well, think about this then. Wayne's taking me
               out tonight. Meal, then a club.

BOB   Very nice. Have a good time.

LINDA   Is that all you've got to say?

BOB   Yes, I think so. You've got your purse with you I
               hope.

               (LINDA *moves off to make herself another coffee.*
               LEONARD *has now got* DAVID *trapped in a corner.*)

LEONARD   . . . That's the trick behind a good talk you see.
               Always capture the attention of the audience
               within the first half an hour; otherwise, you've
               lost them and you'll never get them back. They'll
               make any excuse to get away.

DAVID   (*desperately*) That's fascinating, Leonard . . . you
               must tell me more about it some time. You'll just
               have to excuse me . . . I'm sure I can smell
               something burning in the kitchen.

               (DAVID *escapes from* LEONARD *and is heaving a
               sigh of relief when he gets pounced upon by*
               HELEN.)

HELEN   David, I was wondering whether you might give
               me a lift home tonight?

DAVID   I'd love to Helen but . . .

HELEN   Good. Perhaps we could call in somewhere and
               have a nice little chat?

DAVID   But the thing is Helen, I've already promised to
               give Sue a lift . . . sorry.

HELEN   That's alright, David. We can drop her and then
               go on somewhere . . . (*Making a pathetic attempt*

to flutter her eyelashes.) I'm in no particular rush.

(LEONARD *has spotted that* DAVID *has got side tracked. He goes towards the kitchen.*)

DAVID   But I'm afraid I've got a prior engagement. Sorry and all that but I . . .

LEONARD   (*as he passes* DAVID) It's alright, David, I'll check.

DAVID   Right . . . thanks. (*To* HELEN.) Sorry . . . I was saying I can't let people down. Sorry.

HELEN   (*hurt*) That's quite alright, David . . . I understand.

DAVID   (*feeling guilty*) Look, I'll give you a lift home but then I'll have to dash straight off with Sue . . . to take her home. Excuse me . . . I'll just tell Sue. Alright?

(DAVID *hurries away to* SUE. LEONARD *is in the kitchen with* LINDA.)

LEONARD   (*to* LINDA) I think there's a fire in here somewhere!

LINDA   I can't smell anything. Only a rat. (*She looks over towards* BOB.)

LEONARD   Oh no, I think you'll find it's some kind of combustion.

(LEONARD *and* LINDA *start inspecting the kitchen.*)

DAVID   (*to* SUE) That was close!

SUE   Helen?

DAVID   She wanted to make it a happy threesome!

SUE   I'd have enjoyed that!

DAVID   This is turning into a nightmare. If it's not her it's
            Leonard.

SUE   All you need is Wayne for the complete set!

            (WAYNE *comes up to* SUE.)

WAYNE   Excuse me, Sue, but you don't have any spare
            cash do you . . . I'd pay you back.

            (LINDA *and* LEONARD *have stopped searching and
            are looking over the counter.*)

LEONARD   There's no smoke without fire you know!

LINDA   (*exasperated*) Leonard, we have just looked . . .
            there isn't any fire.

LEONARD   No . . . you've got me misconstrued. Sue and
            David. There's something going on.

            (LEONARD *leaves the kitchen and wanders over to*
            HELEN. SUE *is getting some money out of her bag.*)

SUE   (*to* WAYNE) Five pounds. That's all I can spare.

WAYNE   No, that's great. I wonder if you could do me
            another favour when you get home . . . it's just to
            ring my Mum and let her know I'll be a bit late.

LEONARD   (*to* HELEN) I was just saying . . . there's something
            going on there.

HELEN   Where?

LEONARD   David and Sue. You see if I'm not right.

HELEN   What a ridiculous thought. I can assure you that
            there is absolutely nothing going on at all. David
            and I have a certain understanding.

LEONARD   I think you'll find you're wrong there. I've been
            watching those two for some time.

HELEN   Well in that case you are a very dirty old man
             with an over-fertile imagination!

             (LEONARD *wanders over to continue work on his
             coach.* KATH *enters from the changing room.*)

KATH   May I have everybody's attention please . . .
             thank you. Evonne is extremely upset but I've
             finally persuaded her to carry on. (*There is
             silence for several seconds.*) Alright . . . I know
             that we aren't all entirely happy with the way
             things are going, but we do owe it to Evonne. We
             said that we'd do it and I think we ought to stick
             by that, regardless of how we feel. Evonne is
             trying very hard and at least she's enthusiastic,
             even if she does lack a little . . . experience.

HELEN   And ability!

KATH   That sort of comment isn't very helpful, Helen.

HELEN   Why? I'm only saying what everybody else is
             thinking. I'm sorry, Katherine, but I've always
             been one to call a spade a spade. That woman is
             incompetent.

SUE   I think Kath's right. We've got to carry on.

KATH   What about the rest of you?

             (*There is a general murmur of reluctant
             agreement.*)

             So we carry on then?

BOB   I don't know whether I can stand the pace.
             Compared with this, watching paint dry could
             become a booming leisure activity!

KATH   Thank you, Bob. What about you, Helen?

HELEN   (*reluctant*) I must say that I find your so called
             loyalty rather pitiful. The whole thing is a
             shambles. Nevertheless, against my far superior
             judgement, I will continue . . . just don't expect
             me to enjoy it!

KATH   Helen, I don't think I could ever accuse you of
            enjoying anything!

HELEN   (*indignant*) And exactly what do you mean by
            that?

KATH   (*pleasantly*) Just making an observation, Helen.
            We can all use spades to dig up unpleasant
            truths!

            (HELEN *is not sure how to react.* EVONNE *enters
            hesitantly from the changing room.*)

            (*singing*) For she's a jolly good fellow . . .

            (*The rest of them join in except for* HELEN *who
            can't quite bring herself to do it.*)

EVONNE   (*rather overwhelmed*) I don't quite know what to
            say. I promise that I'll try very hard. Perhaps we
            could get on with the rehearsal . . . alright, super.

KATH   Which part would you like to do, Evonne?

EVONNE   Oh . . . I'm not quite sure. What about the last bit,
            from Cinders trying on the slipper?

SUE   Could we do it in here, please . . . it's freezing on
            that stage.

EVONNE   (*cheerfully*) Yes, what a good idea. It is rather
            cold in there isn't it. I must have a word with
            Donal about it. (*Confidentially.*) His boiler's
            rather past it. Could we just move these chairs out
            of the way?

            (*The chairs are moved back and the cast line up,
            grabbing copies of their scripts. The only
            exception is* LEONARD, *who carries on working.*)

            Super . . . are we all ready? . . . and . . . action.

(They all stand in complete silence. Gradually they all look at WAYNE.)

Cut!

HELEN   You can't "cut" . . . we haven't started yet!

KATH   I think it should have been you, Wayne.

WAYNE   *(surprised)* Oh, right, no problem . . . I didn't think you were ready. WHY AREN'T YOU GOING TO THE BALL, CINDERS?

EVONNE   Cut!

WAYNE   What was wrong with that?

EVONNE   *(apologetically)* Wrong act, actually. Cinders is about to try on the slipper.

WAYNE   Fine . . . why didn't you say! WHY DON'T YOU TRY THE SLIPPER, CINDERS?

HELEN   WHAT, HER!

SUE   YES. I VOWED TO LET EVERY GIRL IN THE LAND TRY IT ON . . . THE SLIPPER. *(To* LINDA.) ARE YOU WILLING?

KATH   *(with feeling)* She's always willing!

          *(*LINDA *and* BOB *glare at* KATH *who glares back. There is a pause for several seconds They all realize that* LEONARD *is missing.)*

SUE   Leonard, it's you!

LEONARD   Is it? I didn't think I was in this bit.

          *(*LEONARD *joins the line up and stands smiling cheerfully at the rest of them.)*

KATH   *(after a few seconds)* Go on then, Leonard!

LEONARD   Oh . . . words as well? *(He opens his mouth a couple of times as if to speak.)* I've misplaced my script.

(EVONNE *gives her script to* LEONARD *and points out the place.*)

Right. YES, TRY IT CINDERS. DON'T YOU THINK SHE SHOULD TRY IT PUSS?

DAVID   MIAOW, MIAOW.

LINDA   VERY WELL. I WILL TRY THE SLIPPER!

WAYNE   IT FITS.

SUE   (*glowering at* WAYNE) I haven't put it on her yet!

            (SUE *pretends to put a slipper on* LINDA'S *foot.*)

ALL   IT FITS!

SUE   IT FITS . . . SUPER.

            (EVONNE *mimes to* SUE *that she should slap her thigh.*)

            SUPER. (*She winces as she slaps her thigh.*)

BOB   If it didn't fit we could end it there. Better still, what if she never got to the ball . . . we could be in the pub by eight!

KATH   Bob!

SUE   AS SOON AS I SAW YOU, I KNEW. WILL YOU MARRY ME?

LINDA   YES . . . YES I WILL MARRY YOU.

SUE   SUPER. (*She slaps her thighs again with a pained expression.*)

HELEN   BUT IT CAN'T BE HER! SHE'S MUCH TOO UGLY.

BOB   YES, I'M MUCH PRETTIER THAN HER . . . AND YOU. (*Pointing at* HELEN.)

HELEN   OH NO YOU'RE NOT.

BOB   OH YES I AM.

HELEN   OH NO YOU'RE NOT.

BOB   (*hitting* HELEN *lightly on the arm*) OH YES I AM.

HELEN   (*hitting* BOB *as hard as she can*) OH NO YOU'RE NOT.

BOB   Ouch . . . Bloody hell. (*He rubs his arm.*)

             (*There is a few seconds silence.*)

EVONNE   Baron.

LEONARD   OH, MY LITTLE GIRL . . . MARRYING A PRINCESS . . . A PRINCE! SUPER. (*He slaps his thigh and looks enthusiastically at* EVONNE.)

SUE   YES, ISN'T IT SUPER. (*Apologetically.*) Could I just mention something, Evonne?

EVONNE   Yes, what is it, Sue?

SUE   Well, it's just that we've noticed that we all seem to keep saying "super" rather a lot. Do you think perhaps we ought to tone it down a little bit . . . cut one or two of them out?

EVONNE   (*earnestly*) But it adds realism to the script, Sue. I mean it's the sort of thing people say isn't it.

KATH   But perhaps if we just cut a few of them out, Evonne. It does seem to crop up rather a lot. I mean, we all say it.

DAVID   (*sulking*) I don't. All I ever say is "miaow"!

KATH   But everybody else does!

EVONNE   (*hurt*) Alright then, if you think it's too much you'd better cut them all out.

KATH   (*hurriedly*) We could say it a few times.

EVONNE   (*bravely*) No . . . no . . . if you all want to change
              my script, that's alright. I don't mind a bit. No
              more "supers" . . . right, shall we carry on? . . .
              super.

              (*They all look rather guilty except for* HELEN *who
              is gloating.*)

SUE   It's you, Wayne.

WAYNE   I know. I'M SO HAPPY FOR YOU, CINDERS.
              WHAT DO YOU SAY, PUSS?

DAVID   MIAOW . . . that's all I ever bloody say!

KATH   AND SO OUR PANTO NEARS ITS END
              AND THEN OUR LEAVE WE'LL TAKE.
              WE HAVEN'T TIME TO HANG AROUND
              A CAKE WE'VE GOT TO BAKE . . . FOR THE
                                               WEDDING.
              THE UGLY SISTERS HAVE BEEN BEAT
              AND GOOD PREVAILS AGAIN
              WE THINK THEY'VE GOT WHAT THEY
                                               DESERVE
              THEY REALLY ARE A PAIN.
              AND SO WE'LL LEAVE YOU WITH A SONG
              TO SEND YOU ON YOUR WAY.
              WE HOPE YOU'VE HAD A SUPER TIME
              AND WILL COME BACK AGAIN . . . NEXT YEAR.

EVONNE   So then the fairy disappears in a puff of smoke . . .

BOB   We should be so lucky!

              (KATH *hits him with her script which she has been
              using as a wand.*)

EVONNE   And then curtain closes . . . curtain opens . . . and
              straight into the final song . . .

              (*She switches on the portable cassette player. As
              they sing their individual lines, each of the cast*

does a mime: KATH *waves her wand and does a pirouette.* WAYNE *wipes tears from his eyes.* HELEN *preens herself.* BOB *exaggerates the size of his stomach.* LEONARD *waves his arms about, not knowing what to do.* DAVID *cleans his whiskers.* SUE *places her hands on her heart.* LINDA *indicates an imaginary wedding ring on her finger.*)

Verse 1

ALL   WHEN YOU'RE AT THE PANTOMIME
        A HAPPY ENDING'S BRILL
        BUT THINGS WOULD HAVE TURNED OUT
                            MUCH WORSE
        WITHOUT THE FAIRY'S SKILL
        NOW CINDERELLA'S GOT HER PRINCE
        HER SISTERS END WITH NIL
        AND PUSSY'S GOT HIS BOWL OF MILK
        SO HE CAN DRINK HIS FILL

Chorus

        WASN'T IT A SUPER DAY
        WE'VE HAD A SUPER TIME
        WE'LL HAVE A SUPER WEDDING
        LOTS OF SONG AND DANCE AND WINE
        THE BELLS WILL RING REJOICING
        AND THE SUN IS BOUND TO SHINE
        AND SO WE SAY FAREWELL
        TO THIS MOST SUPER PANTOMIME.

Verse 2

KATH   I'M THE FAIRY N'ERE CONTRARY
        SEE MY MAGIC'S FINE
WAYNE   I'M CINDERS' FRIEND AND IN THE END
        WISH CINDERS COULD BE MINE
HELEN   AND I'M A SISTER DEVIOUS TWISTER
        THOUGH I LOOK DIVINE
BOB   SHE'S OFF HER NUT HER BEER GUT
        IS TWICE AS BIG AS MINE

HELEN   (*angrily*) That isn't in the script!

Verse 3

LEONARD   SHE'S MY DAUGHTER AND I TAUGHT HER
            EVERYTHING SHE KNOWS
DAVID   I'M CINDERS' CAT AND OFTEN SAT
            WHILE CINDERS DARNED HER CLOTHES
SUE   AND I'M PRINCE CHARMING IT'S ALARMING
            JUST HOW QUICK LOVE GROWS
LINDA   I'LL BE HIS WIFE AND PLEDGE MY LIFE
            TO FOLLOW WHERE HE GOES

            (*Repeat Chorus.*)

            (*Repeat verses two and three together, singing
            over each other.*)

            (*Repeat Chorus.*)

EVONNE   (*as the final line fades*) Super!

            (*Curtain falls.*)

ACT TWO

Scene One

Three weeks later and it is half an hour before curtain up on the first night of the pantomime. KATH, SUE *and* EVONNE *are talking.* KATH *is already changed into her fairy costume. It is fairly amateurish as are all the costumes, consisting of a white tutu, liberal amounts of tinsel and a silver wand.* SUE *is dressed as Prince Charming, with a tunic, tights and boots.* BOB, *who is not yet changed, is sitting apart from the others and studying his script. Various props are scattered around the room, including a large wash tub which is mounted on wheels to make it transportable.* LEONARD'S *coach is covered over with a dust sheet.*

EVONNE   (*tearfully*) What am I going to do! I knew it was going to be a disaster . . . I told you.

KATH   When did she ring?

EVONNE   I don't know . . . it's all just a blur. About two hours ago.

KATH   And think carefully . . . are you sure you didn't get it mixed up? What did she say exactly?

EVONNE   (*thinking very hard*) She said . . . she said that the whole thing was a shambles . . . a total shambles . . . and that she wasn't going to belittle herself by being involved any longer.

KATH   And that's all?

EVONNE   Yes . . . well she used a lot of other words that I think were rather rude . . . I'd never heard some of them.

KATH   (*turning on* BOB) Do something.

     (BOB *ignores her.*)

     Bob!

BOB   Sorry, I didn't realize you were talking to me. I thought a cockroach or something must have crawled in.

| KATH | No it hasn't, so unfortunately you'll have to do! Do something about Helen . . . she's taken her woggle home. |

BOB I'd have thought that would be a relief to everybody.

SUE It's opening night, Bob. We're short of an ugly sister.

BOB Well that means there's a spare ticket for the ball. If Cinders uses that, we don't need a fairy either.

KATH Thank you, Bob. (*Thinking.*) There's only one way round it . . . you'll have to do it, Evonne.

EVONNE (*shocked*) What?

SUE Yeah, that's a great idea. You'd be alright.

EVONNE No . . . I can't. I'd be dreadful. I can't go on the stage . . . people might look at me!

SUE You'd be fine. She'd be great wouldn't she, Bob?

BOB Yeah, why not. You'd be a much better ugly sister than Helen . . . you're a natural.

EVONNE What? How do you mean a natural?

BOB (*realizing his mistake*) Pardon? . . . No, I didn't mean . . . that you're a natural ugly . . . just better at it than Helen.

(EVONNE *starts sobbing.*)

No . . . by better I didn't mean more ugly than her . . . you're the same . . . better!

SUE (*coming to the rescue*) Bob means that you're a better actress, don't you, Bob?

BOB Yes . . . I'm sure that's what I was trying to say!

(BOB *returns thankfully to his lines.*)

EVONNE	Oh, it's awful . . . I don't know the lines . . . I don't know anything!
KATH	(*firmly*) Come on. Let's get you sorted out. You'll be alright . . . just don't panic.

(KATH *leads* EVONNE *out to the changing room.*)

EVONNE	I think I feel sick!
SUE	Don't panic! That's like telling a fish to stop swimming.
BOB	What?
SUE	I said it's like . . . (*Giving up.*) Shouldn't you be getting changed? We're on in twenty minutes.
BOB	Soon. I'm just doing a bit of last minute swatting.
SUE	Why bother now? You haven't stuck to the script in rehearsals. Anyway, I'd have thought you'd had plenty of time to learn it at home.
BOB	How's that?
SUE	Doesn't peace still reign supreme in your house? . . . not talking . . . you and Kath.
BOB	(*miserable*) Oh, we're still not talking but that's hardly the same as peace. A well timed silence is worth hours of shouting!
SUE	You mean it's getting worse?
BOB	What finally did it was when she found out that Linda went to the conference. Up until then she'd just been annoyed. Now it's far worse . . . she's hurt.
SUE	(*impatient*) So why did you do it? You knew how she felt.
BOB	But I didn't do it! I told Linda she couldn't go, then my boss over-ruled me.
SUE	So you didn't want her to go?

BOB   Course I wanted her to go . . . it's just that for
           once I was actually thinking of Kath.

SUE   And nothing happened . . . when you were there?

BOB   No it didn't. It could have, but it didn't. That's
           the galling thing about it. The way Kath's acting I
           might just as well have . . . enjoyed myself.

SUE   So why haven't you explained all that to Kath?
           She'd understand.

BOB   (*frustrated*) She doesn't want to understand!
           Look, she thinks that I fancy Linda, which I do . . .
           and that I'm chasing after her, which I'm not.
           But that's what she wants to believe, so . . . end
           of story.

SUE   Don't be stupid, Bob. Why would she want to
           believe that? It's crazy.

BOB   Is it? Things haven't been right between us for
           ages . . . we're just going through one of those
           phases. Whenever we've tried to talk we just end
           up getting annoyed with each other . . . I sulk and
           she throws things! Now Kath's found the perfect
           answer. Something to . . . I don't know . . . focus
           all her frustration on. That's not crazy . . . it's sad
           but it's not crazy.

SUE   Do you want me to talk to her?

BOB   But then she'd just get annoyed with you. She'd
           think you were interfering. Worse still that I'd
           been moaning to you.

SUE   Come on, I know Kath better than that. Maybe
           she needs to talk to somebody. Look I'll try to
           catch her when she's on her own sometime . . .
           alright?

BOB   (*dejected but forcing a smile*) It's all my fault you
           know. I always thought that as I got older I'd
           know exactly what I wanted out of life. It doesn't

happen that way though does it? I mean, the grass
is still greener on the other side of the fence . . .
it's just that you notice all the nettles as well. I
suppose it gets to the stage where you can't even
manage to climb over . . . you just stand there
peeping through . . . wondering if you made the
right decision.

SUE   Do you still love Kath?

BOB   Course I do. I always will. I'm just not very good
at showing it.

(LEONARD *enters with* LINDA. *He is dressed in his
Baron Hardup costume but somehow looks as
dishevelled as he always does. He is carrying his
suitcase.*)

LEONARD   Good evening all.

BOB   }   Hi.
SUE   Hi.

LINDA   Hello, Sue. (*She pointedly ignores* BOB.) Ready
for the big event?

SUE   I've started getting the jitters already. I don't
know why I got myself into this.

BOB   Snap! How do you feel, Linda?

LINDA   (*acidly*) Does it matter? I thought you had no
further interest in me!

BOB   Come on, Linda, it's not like that. We can still be
friends can't we?

LINDA   I'm very choosy about my friends.

LEONARD   (*producing an ancient camera from his suitcase*)
Would you just stand over there please. I want to
start getting a few pictures . . . for my archives as
I like to call them.

BOB   They're not going to form the nucleus of talk
               number seventeen thousand are they? I don't think
               I want to be reduced to a catalogue number.

LEONARD   Oh, I don't want you yet. I'm not wasting film on
               you . . . you're not dressed. I just want people in
               their costumes. (*To* SUE.) Now, if you could just
               pose.

BOB   It's the boots and tights! I'd watch yourself, Sue.

LEONARD   Could you say cheese please?

BOB   (*to* LEONARD) Did you come on your bike like that?

LEONARD   Yes. Just one or two more, if you don't mind.

LINDA   I'm going to get changed.

SUE   Go on, Bob, you need to get changed as well.

LINDA   Yes, perhaps you could change into a nicer
               person!

               (LINDA *exits to the changing room and* BOB *rises
               to follow her.*)

SUE   Do I notice an air of discontent there as well?

BOB   I had a talk with her yesterday . . . I think it's
               called burning your bridges.

               (BOB *exits.* LEONARD *continues to bumble around
               happily.*)

SUE   You're really enjoying all this aren't you? . . . the
               pantomime.

LEONARD   It's alright, yes. It makes a nice change . . .
               something a bit different. Fills the time in.

SUE   I'd have thought you had enough on your plate
               already, what with all your talks. Doesn't Mrs
               Trotter mind you being out so much?

LEONARD   (*sadly*) There isn't a Mrs Trotter. I lost her five
               years ago.

SUE   Oh, I'm sorry . . . I didn't realize. I just sort of
           assumed . . .

LEONARD   Oh, that's alright. (*Reminiscing.*) She was a fine
           woman. It was on her birthday you know . . . that
           she went. It was all very sudden . . . no warning at
           all really. Still, I expect she's far happier where
           she is now.

SUE   (*comforting*) Yes . . . yes I'm sure she is.

LEONARD   Of course it was very hard at first. It takes a lot of
           adjustment you know. All you've got left is
           memories of happier days . . . photographs and
           memories. It's very difficult to come to terms
           with. There was many a time when I'd go and
           stand on the flyover near our house and think . . .
           should I take the plunge . . . should I go after her.

SUE   (*almost in tears*) I'm glad you didn't . . . that's
           not the answer is it.

LEONARD   No, that's what I thought . . . it's a long way to
           Milton Keynes.

SUE   What?

LEONARD   Milton Keynes. That's where she went . . . with
           the insurance man. She said he was more
           interesting than me.

SUE   You mean she's still . . . she's not . . . I thought
           you meant, you know.

LEONARD   I suppose I ought to have known something was
           going on, but you never really think do you? I
           should have had suspicions though . . . he came
           round for his premium four nights a week!
           (*Pause.*) Still, best get on. (*Pointing to the
           coach.*) Few last minute touches.

           (LEONARD *wanders over to the coach and removes
           the dust sheet. The coach is virtually finished,
           but is as unprofessional and unrealistic as could*

be imagined. SUE *looks at it in dismay as* LEONARD *starts to work on it.* WAYNE *enters from the car park.*)

WAYNE   Hi.

SUE   Where have you been? You'd better get changed quick!

WAYNE   Ah . . . slight problem. I just came round to say I was going to have to give it a miss.

SUE   What? (*Furious.*) You can't back out now, Wayne . . . everybody's depending on you!

WAYNE   Sorry . . . I'm ill.

SUE   What do you mean, ill. You look well enough to me.

WAYNE   (*putting on a strained voice*) Yeah, well I've been trying to fight it off, you know. I think it's a recurrence of one of these tropical diseases. I get a lot of problems with them. I mean, you look great but you feel terrible.

SUE   Come off it Wayne! You've never been near the tropics in your life.

WAYNE   (*indignant*) As it happens, that's where you're wrong. I've been to the Costa Brava loads of times . . . and France.

SUE   Oh, that's it then! The only person who's ever caught yellow fever in the Costa Brava.

LEONARD   Excuse me, but I made a study of tropical diseases for one of my talks. I think you'll find . . . and I'm sure I'm right on this one . . . that you don't get any wide spread out breaks of tropical diseases in Spain. It's not a tropical climate, you see.

WAYNE   (*patiently*) Yeah, I know that, but I'm not talking about Spain am I . . . everyone's been to Spain. I'm talking about the Costa Brava.

LEONARD   But the Costa Brava . . .

SUE   It's alright, Mr Trotter, any explanation would be
           totally lost on Wayne. I was wrong about the
           yellow fever . . . he hasn't got a fever . . . he's
           just plain yellow!

WAYNE   Me?

SUE   It's called stage fright, Wayne. I've got it . . .
           we've all got it . . . the only difference is that we
           don't give in as easily as you.

WAYNE   Hey . . . me . . . with stage fright! I don't know
           the meaning of the word fear.

SUE   You don't know the meaning of most words,
           Wayne, but try these out . . . scared . . . terrified .
           . . cowardly. Any of those ring a bell? You've lost
           your bottle!

WAYNE   (*defiant*) Ok, I'll show you who's scared . . . you
           just try and keep me off that stage!

SUE   (*smiling sweetly*) You're so predictable, Wayne,
           do you know that?

LEONARD   I haven't got stage fright.

SUE   (*patiently*) Probably because you can never find
           your way onto the stage, Leonard.

           (KATH *enters, dragging a reluctant* EVONNE *behind
           her.* EVONNE *is wearing* HELEN'S *"ugly sister"
           costume and* BOB'S *wig. She is heavily made up,
           with bright red lips and cheeks.*)

KATH   Well . . . what do you think?

           (WAYNE *has a quick glance over at* EVONNE *and
           mistakes her for* BOB.)

WAYNE   Hi, Bob.

KATH   (*before* EVONNE *can protest*) It's not Bob, it's
           Evonne! Don't you think she looks good?

WAYNE   Oh . . . yeah, great. I've never seen you with make
             up on, Evonne you should use it more often.

KATH   She's in the panto, Wayne! She's standing in for
             Helen. Do you think she looks ugly enough?

WAYNE   (*confused*) Yeah, fine . . . especially if you get
             that make up off her . . . it'll be great.

EVONNE   (*unable to contain herself*) But I'm trying to be
             ugly!

WAYNE   (*reassuringly*) No problem.

EVONNE   I can't do it . . . he thought I was Bob! We'll have
             to cancel.

KATH   Don't be silly, Evonne . . . you'll be fine. Here,
             sit down and take the weight off your nerves.

SUE   I'll make you a cup of tea . . . calm you down.

             (SUE *goes into the kitchen as* KATH *surveys the
             scene.*)

KATH   Right, how's everybody doing? You'd better get
             ready, Wayne.

WAYNE   (*having second thoughts*) Yeah . . . fine, no
             problem. (*As he exits to the changing room.*) I'm
             not sure whether I can go on though.

KATH   (*to* LEONARD) What's all that about?

LEONARD   I believe he's lost a bottle of some sort.

SUE   (*shouting from the kitchen*) He's just got nerves.

KATH   I must admit, I'm getting a few butterflies myself.

SUE   Have you had that dream yet?

KATH   What dream?

SUE   Well, I think it's probably more of a nightmare
             really . . . you must have had it, everybody does.

You're standing in the wings, Ok, and you know that you've got to go on in a couple of minutes, but you can't remember any of your lines . . . you can't even remember what the play is about or anything . . . you don't even know who you're supposed to be!

EVONNE   (*miserably*) I feel like that now and I'm awake!

(LEONARD, *un-noticed by* EVONNE, *has lined up to take a photograph of her.*)

LEONARD   Smile please.

(*The flash goes off and* EVONNE, *who is totally unexpecting it, nearly falls off her chair.*)

Thank you.

KATH   I think perhaps you should put that down for the moment, Leonard, we're not quite up to it. Are you alright, Evonne?

EVONNE   (*flustered*) I think so . . . the flash just took me by surprise . . . I thought I was starting a migraine.

LEONARD   Well I think I'll just go round to the front of our house as we call it in the theatre . . . I'd like to get a few shots of the audience and such like . . . I like to get a balanced record.

(LEONARD *heads for the door to the car park.*)

KATH   You can't go round like that!

LEONARD   No, I'll be alright, it's not cold . . . in fact I believe I'm right in saying that it's unseasonably mild at present . . . for the season, that is . . . I heard it on the BBC weather.

KATH   That's not what I meant! You're in costume . . . it's not professional.

LEONARD   Well, neither am I!

(*Before* KATH *can stop him* LEONARD *exits to the car park.*)

KATH   I give up! (*Pointing to the coach.*) And have you seen the state of that!

SUE   He's done his best. At least it's kept him occupied.

KATH   But Cinderella's supposed to be moving up in the world. As chief fairy, I'd say it's a waste of a good pumpkin!

EVONNE   (*pitifully*) I feel sick again! I think it was that light flashing in my eyes.

SUE   Don't worry, Evonne, it'll soon pass. Here's your tea, that'll make you feel better.

            (SUE *fetches a mug of tea out of the kitchen and gives it to* EVONNE.)

EVONNE   Thank you. I'm sorry to be such a pest. Donal says that I'm a pest sometimes. I don't know what he's going to say after this though. It's going to be a total failure.

KATH   Of course it isn't!

            (BOB *enters from the changing room. He is changed into his costume and make up, but is not wearing a wig.*)

BOB   Well?

            (SUE *bursts out laughing.*)

            What's wrong with it!

KATH   Don't worry, Bob We were just talking about failures!

EVONNE   It will be . . . I know. What happens if the audience just sits in complete silence all the way through it? . . . worse still, what if they all get up and walk out during the interval! (*Panicking*.) Do you think we should cancel the interval?

BOB   Course not . . . it's the best bit!

KATH   Bob! Calm down, Evonne . . . I'm sure there won't be a mass walk out.

BOB   Yeah, it's impossible.

EVONNE   (*brightening*) Do you think so?

BOB   I know so. I don't think four people constitutes a mass. I had a peep through the curtain.

EVONNE   Only four?

BOB   Afraid so . . . that's if you count Donal and the tea lady.

EVONNE   I knew it!

KATH   (*cheerfully*) Well, Leonard's going round . . . that'll make five . . . temporarily.

SUE   Anyway there's lot's of time yet . . . ten minutes! It'll fill up, won't it, Bob.

BOB   Oh, bound to. I've got a couple of girls coming from work.

KATH   (*accusingly*) You didn't tell me.

BOB   You didn't ask! Anyway, I mean girl in the loosest sense.

KATH   But that's the type of girl you like isn't it!

SUE   (*jumping in before an argument develops*) Where's your wig Bob?

BOB   Evonne's wearing it.

SUE   You'll have to use Helen's. It's in the dressing room I think, in her corner.

BOB   Which is her corner . . . oh, never mind . . . I'll
              look for her broom stick. (*As he exits*.) Unless
              Kath parked hers in there as well!

KATH   One of these days I am going to swing for him!

              (DAVID *enters hurriedly from the car park*.)

SUE   (*concerned*) Where have you been . . . I was
              beginning to think something had happened to
              you!

DAVID   I called for Helen. She rang me up and said that
              she'd ducked out, so I thought I'd better do my
              bit. It took me longer than I thought.

SUE   You mean she's coming?

DAVID   I gave her a lift down. (*He glances around and
              sees* EVONNE.) Hey, Bob, that looks good.

              (EVONNE *looks round, horrified*.)

              Bob!

EVONNE   It's me!

KATH   It's Evonne.

DAVID   Oh . . . sorry . . . why are you . . .

EVONNE   I don't look like Bob do I?

DAVID   What? . . . no, of course you don't.

EVONNE   You thought I was Bob!

DAVID   No . . . you don't look a bit like Bob. I mean he
              probably looks a bit like you . . . with a frock and
              everything.

EVONNE   (*wailing*) I look like Bob!

KATH   You don't . . . you don't at all.

              (HELEN *marches in purposefully from the car park*.)

HELEN   Before anyone says a single word, I would like to
          make it quite clear that I am only here under
          extreme protest. It's only due to David's heart felt
          pleas that I have decided to appear after all.
          Furthermore I would stress that —

KATH   Just who do you think you are! You waltz in
          here . . .

HELEN   If you would let me finish —

KATH   No! You waltz in here with your nose up in the air
          as though we all owe you a huge favour or
          something.

HELEN   As I was saying . . . I would stress that I am
          certainly not here for Evonne's sake. Where is the
          stupid little woman anyway?

EVONNE   (*with as much dignity as she can muster*) I'm
          here!

HELEN   (*shocked*) What are you doing dressed like that . . .
          I thought you were Bob. You look ridiculous!

KATH   She's meant to look ridiculous . . . she's standing
          in for you.

HELEN   She's what!

KATH   Watch my lips . . . she's standing in for you. We
          don't need you to go on stage. So why don't you
          take over her jobs and see how you like that.

HELEN   Her jobs!

KATH   Yes. Curtains, props . . .

EVONNE   (*miserably*) Lights.

KATH   Lights.

EVONNE   Scenery.

KATH   Scenery . . . prompt.

EVONNE   Prompt.

KATH   (*amazed*) Are you sure you're doing all those?

EVONNE   (*even more miserable*) I couldn't get anyone.

HELEN   See what I mean? Gross inefficiency. Tell them,
                David.

DAVID   Sorry, just dashing . . . I need to get ready.

                (DAVID *tries to escape to the changing room.*)

HELEN   (*forcefully*) David . . . I came along here expressly
                at your wish. Now, tell them that I'm better than
                her.

EVONNE   There isn't any need . . .

HELEN   Evonne, please . . . this is nothing to do with you.
                David?

DAVID   Well . . . I think . . . I think that it would be really
                good if we had three ugly sisters . . . make it a bit
                different.

HELEN   Stop hedging, David.

SUE   You did let us down, Helen. It was very brave of
                Evonne to volunteer.

EVONNE   But I didn't volunteer.

KATH   My vote goes to Evonne.

HELEN   Yes, well I would expect that from you. David?

DAVID   I don't know. Look, as you don't really want to do
                it and Evonne does, wouldn't it be more sensible
                to let Evonne go on?

EVONNE   But I don't want to . . .

HELEN   Evonne, I've asked you before to stop interrupting.
                So you've turned against me as well have you,
                David?

DAVID   I'm not turning against anybody.

EVONNE   (*finally losing her temper and shouting*) Will you
            all just listen to me! (*Embarrassed at herself.*) I
            don't want to do it . . . I didn't volunteer. Now
            that Helen's here, she ought to go on.

SUE   Are you sure, Evonne?

EVONNE   Of course I am.

HELEN   Well I'm pleased to see that you at least have
            come to your senses, Evonne . . . although I don't
            know why you didn't speak out earlier . . . it
            would have saved all this unnecessary argument.
            I'll go and prepare myself. Evonne, I need those
            clothes. (*As she exits to the changing room.*) I
            shall speak to you later, David!

KATH   (*to* EVONNE) You don't have to give in to her you
            know.

EVONNE   I've got to . . . I'd be hopeless.

            (EVONNE *exits to the changing room.*)

SUE   (*to* DAVID) Looks like you're in Helen's bad
            books!

DAVID   Yeah. I don't know whether to be delighted or
            terrified!

SUE   Don't worry, I'll protect you. (*She kisses* DAVID
            lightly on the lips.) Go on, we'll be starting soon.

DAVID   Ok. (*He kisses* SUE.) See you in a minute. (*He
            exits to the changing room.*)

KATH   Do I detect a hint of romance in the air?

SUE   Whatever gave you that idea? Oh, Kath . . .
            (*Reaching out and hugging* KATH.) . . . I've never
            been so happy! I'm walking on air at the moment.

KATH   Well, it has been a little obvious for the last few
            weeks . . . except to Helen of course! I'm really
            pleased for you.

SUE   Thanks. We were trying to keep it a secret but I
           suppose we didn't do too well. (*After a pause.*)
           Kath, can I talk to you?

KATH   Yes, of course.

SUE   (*hesitantly*) It's about Bob.

KATH   In that case, forget it.

SUE   But, Kath, there are some things you don't know.
           I like you and Bob and I hate to see you like this
           . . . it wouldn't do any harm to listen would it?

KATH   (*suspicious*) Did Bob put you up to this?

SUE   No he didn't. Look, we've got time for a quick
           coffee . . . just listen.

           (SUE *guides a reluctant* KATH *into the kitchen.*)

KATH   This had better be good!

           (LINDA *and* WAYNE *enter from the changing room.
           They are in costume and are going over their
           lines together.*)

LINDA   THANK YOU FOR TALKING TO ME,
           BUTTONS. I WAS SO LONELY.

WAYNE   (*in a macho voice*) HEY, ARE YOU GOING TO
           THE BALL OR WHAT?

LINDA   (*frustrated*) Will you stick to the script!

WAYNE   I was just trying to make him a bit more . . . you
           know, macho.

LINDA   Is that what it was supposed to be? He's not
           meant to be macho . . . he's a wimp! Just act
           normally.

WAYNE   What?

LINDA   No, I mean just do it how you have through the
           rehearsals.

WAYNE   Yeah, Ok . . . Can we sit down . . . I don't feel too good.

       (*They sit.*)

LINDA   It's just nerves, Wayne.

WAYNE   What me? I've been in tighter spots than this! I don't get nerves.

LINDA   Oh come on, you don't have to try the tough guy bit with me. Why try to put on an act all the time?

WAYNE   Me? Hey, I can't help it if I'm a pretty wild guy.

LINDA   Wayne . . . you're about as wild a guy as Leonard! I don't mean that nastily . . . but just be yourself. You don't have to try to impress me you know . . . I prefer what's underneath.

WAYNE   You do?

LINDA   Look . . . I owe you an apology.

WAYNE   What for?

LINDA   That night a few weeks ago . . . when we went out. I was a real bitch, wasn't I?

WAYNE   (*sadly*) Yeah. (*Recovering.*) Hey, there's no need to apologize to me. I can get any number of chicks.

LINDA   Wayne, just shut up for a minute will you? I'm sorry I created a scene in the restaurant . . . I was just a bit surprised when I had to pay the bill.

WAYNE   No it's Ok, I should have told you I was broke . . . it was only temporary mind, I'm usually loaded.

LINDA   No you're not . . . not unless the dole pays better than it used to!

WAYNE   Who told you that?

LINDA   It doesn't matter. I went out with you that night for all the wrong reasons . . . I thought you were a complete idiot . . . but you're not. Not if you'd just be yourself.

WAYNE   Really?

LINDA   I'd like to go out again sometime . . . but not until I know I'm going to get the real Wayne.

WAYNE   You would?

LINDA   Yes . . . I really would.

(LEONARD *enters from the car park*.)

LEONARD   It's really starting to fill up out there!

LINDA   Pardon?

LEONARD   It's filling up . . . in the auditorium.

LINDA   How many?

LEONARD   Oh, there's ten or eleven now. Of course, I'm used to much bigger audiences, with my talks. I once gave a talk to over forty women at a young wives meeting. They left the subject matter up to me so I gave them fuel injection systems for beginners . . . that's one of my favourites. It seemed to go down quite well although they didn't ask many questions. In fact it was quite odd really because previous to the talk they said that they'd probably want me back at another time. They never did get in touch.

LINDA   Perhaps they lost your telephone number.

LEONARD   (*not convinced*) Yes, I expect that's what it was . . I might get in touch with them. I'll take your pictures now you're changed. Could you just pose for me?

LINDA   Wayne poses for everybody. Come on. (LINDA *drapes herself provocatively around* WAYNE. *He is acutely embarrassed.*)

WAYNE   Hey, Linda.

(WAYNE *tries to pull himself away but* LINDA *persists*.)

LINDA   It's only a photograph, Wayne.

KATH   (*looking out at* LINDA) Look . . . she's started on him now!

SUE   But that's what I'm telling you. There's nothing between her and Bob.

LEONARD   Thank you.

LINDA   You'd better sit down again, Wayne.

WAYNE   (*wiping his brow*) Yeah, it's a bit warm isn't it?

LEONARD   (*thinking*) It's very odd you know.

LINDA   What's that?

LEONARD   Well, it's just occurred to me . . . it's never dawned before but I've set myself off thinking . . . I've never had a repeat booking anywhere! It's very strange is that . . . does it seem strange to you? It seems strange to me.

LINDA   Maybe it's just coincidence.

LEONARD   Maybe, but it still seems queer. I mean all my talks are very interesting. I could understand it if they were a bit tedious . . . but they're interesting. I pride myself on that.

LINDA   I'm sure they are.

LEONARD   I like to think of them as stimulating. I'm doing one for the party you know . . . final night party as we call it. I thought I'd give you "The History of Pantomime". I've got to write it yet though . . . I'm currently undertaking research.

LINDA   Very nice.

LEONARD   Illustrated with slides of course.

LINDA   Lovely.

LEONARD   In colour.

LINDA   Super . . . God, I'm saying it now!

            (BOB *enters from the changing room, now wearing his wig.*)

LEONARD   I was just saying . . . I'll do the history of pantomime for you . . . when I've written it.

BOB   Well, I wouldn't write it 'til after tonight. We'll probably set pantomime back about a century!

            (SUE *hurries up to* BOB *as* LEONARD *goes to complete work on the coach.*)

SUE   Bob, Kath's in the kitchen. She'd like a word.

BOB   I bet I know which one!

SUE   Go on quick . . . before you have to go on stage.

BOB   But I was hoping to walk on . . . it'll be embarrassing making an entrance on crutches!

            (BOB *goes reluctantly into the kitchen.*)

            I understand you summoned me.

KATH   (*gently*) Yes, I've got one or two things to say to you. Sue's been talking to me.

BOB   Oh, I'm sorry, Kath . . . I told her not to get involved.

KATH   I'm glad she did! I've been stupid, Bob. (*Hugging him.*) I don't know what to say . . . I'm sorry, I should have trusted you.

BOB   (*stunned*) You mean you believe her . . . believe me?

KATH   Yes, of course I do. (*Suddenly suspicious.*) Is there any reason I shouldn't?

BOB   Of course not. I just didn't think you would somehow.

KATH   I'm sorry.

BOB   I'm sorry as well. I shouldn't have given you any
            reason to feel like you did. Forgive me?

KATH   We should have sorted this out ages ago. I was
            just being obstinate.

BOB   No more than usual. (*He kisses* KATH
            passionately.)

KATH   I've never been kissed by a woman before . . . not
            like that anyway!

BOB   And I've never kissed a fairy. Want to try it again?

KATH   Yes please. Otherwise I'll turn you into a frog!

            (*They are kissing again as* HELEN *enters from the
            changing room. She has changed into her
            costume. As she passes the kitchen door she sees*
            BOB *and* KATH *and watches them for a few
            seconds before continuing in.*)

HELEN   Have you seen those two! It's disgusting, carrying
            on like that!

SUE   They are married you know.

HELEN   That makes it even worse . . . married people of
            their age performing in public . . . it's obscene!

SUE   But they weren't in public, 'til you stopped for a
            gawp.

HELEN   I do not gawp, Susan. Where's David . . . I have a
            bone to pick with him.

SUE   He's still changing I think.

HELEN   Changing? He's avoiding me, that's what he's
            doing. He let me down badly . . . and he knows it.

            (KATH *and* BOB *enter from the kitchen.*)

BOB   (*to* KATH) I think your spell went wrong . . . the
               frog's in here! . . . oh, no, sorry it's Helen. (*To*
               HELEN.) God you look ravishing . . . give us a
               kiss.

               (BOB *advances towards her and* HELEN *backs
               away.*)

HELEN   Don't get any ideas . . . you're not doing that with
               me!

BOB   (*innocently*) What?

HELEN   That . . . in there. I'm not as easy as her.

BOB   Her? . . . oh, her! . . . I'm sorry, Helen, have you
               met my wife.

HELEN   Wife or not, it's disgusting carrying on like that.

KATH   You're only jealous.

HELEN   I can assure you that nothing could be further
               from the truth. I have no wish to be asphyxiated,
               thank you . . . especially by your husband.

KATH   (*hackles rising*) And what is wrong with my
               husband! You'd be lucky to get anybody near you
               . . . married or not.

               (DAVID *enters from the changing room He is
               dressed in black and has large whiskers, ears,
               nose and a tail.*)

HELEN   How dare you say that to me!

KATH   It's quite easy, because it's true. Why don't you
               ask David.

HELEN   What is she talking about, David?

DAVID   I don't know . . . I've just walked in.

HELEN   She is making insinuations about my . . . my . . .
               me!

BOB   (*trying to calm things*) I think you've gone a bit
           far, Kath.

KATH   She deserves it!

HELEN   (*to* DAVID) Well . . . do something!

DAVID   What am I supposed to do?

HELEN   Demand an apology. If I don't get an apology I'm
           leaving.

SUE   You can't do that . . . we're on in a minute!

HELEN   You may well be on . . . I will be off.

KATH   You can say that again!

SUE   I'm sorry, Helen, but maybe you should be the one
           to apologize. After all, it was you who started it.

HELEN   And I shall finish it as well . . . by walking out of
           here.

WAYNE   Clear off then . . . we don't need an old bag like
           you!

HELEN   How dare you speak to me like that! (*Turning for
           support.*) David!

DAVID   (*reluctant to get involved*) You shouldn't have
           said that, Wayne.

WAYNE   Why not? She is!

HELEN   David . . . hit him!

           (WAYNE *quickly dodges behind* LINDA.)

DAVID   I'm a police officer . . . I can't just go around
           hitting people!

BOB   (*joking*) I thought it was an integral part of the
           job!

           (DAVID *glares at him.*)

WAYNE   It's alright, Linda . . . let him past . . . I can take
                 him.

                 (DAVID *holds up his hand to pacify* WAYNE *who
                 crouches further behind* LINDA.)

LINDA   Grow up, Wayne.

WAYNE   No . . . he's getting me going now. You just let
                 him make a move!

SUE   Just stop it, all of you.

KATH   Yes, it's between me and Helen.

HELEN   Right . . . well in that case.

                 (HELEN *grabs* KATH'S *wand and breaks it in two
                 across her knee.*)

KATH   That's my wand! You . . .

                 (KATH *pulls* HELEN'S *wig off and throws it on the
                 floor.* HELEN *grabs* KATH'S *tiara and throws it
                 down. They start fighting with each other.*)

WAYNE   (*chanting*) Come on the fairies!

                 (DAVID *grabs* HELEN *and* BOB *grabs* KATH *and the
                 two are dragged apart.*)

BOB   Calm down.

DAVID   That's enough, Helen.

HELEN   It most certainly is . . . Goodbye.

                 (HELEN *marches out to the car park.*)

SUE   Oh no!

                 (*They all stand in stunned silence for a few
                 seconds.* EVONNE *enters cheerfully from the
                 changing room.*)

EVONNE   Two minutes. All ready? Super . . . isn't this nice
                 just like one big happy family. (*She beams around
                 at them all.*) Super.

(EVONNE *spots* KATH *looking sadly at her wand.*)

What's happened to your wand?

KATH   (*sheepishly*) It sort of fell apart in Helen's hand.

LEONARD   It's alright . . . I'll have that as good as new in no time. (*He produces some insulating tape from his suitcase.*) I always carry this in case of accidents and the like.

(LEONARD *takes the wand from* KATH *and starts to repair it, rather untidily.*)

EVONNE   Well done, Leonard . . . curtain up in three minutes everybody. (*With sudden realisation.*) Where is Helen?

KATH   I'm not quite sure how to tell you this but . . . we had a little misunderstanding and she left.

EVONNE   (*horrified*) Not home!

KATH   Home-ish.

EVONNE   What have I been saying all along . . . it's happened . . . it's a disaster!

(*The rest of them stand around looking rather shame-faced.*)

DAVID   (*reluctantly*) It's alright, I'll fetch her back. Neither of us is on for a while. I'm sure I can sweet talk her.

SUE   But will you find her?

DAVID   She won't have gone far . . . I can't see her getting on the bus looking like that!

(DAVID *exits to the car park.*)

EVONNE   (*distraught*) We'll have to cancel . . . send the entire audience home.

BOB   Shall I order them a taxi?

KATH   Bob! Everything's fine, Evonne. Helen *will* come
                back . . . it'll all go smoothly.

EVONNE   Are you sure?

KATH   Of course. (*Although her face reveals that she
                isn't sure at all.*)

                (LEONARD *hands the wand back to* KATH. *It is very
                bent and has tape hanging everywhere.*)

LEONARD   There you are . . . good as new.

KATH   (*surveying it*) Thank you, Leonard . . . very neat!

EVONNE   (*worried*) We'd better make a start then. I'll open
                the curtains so could we have beginners on please.
                Good luck everybody.

BOB   You're not supposed to say that . . . it's bad luck.
                You're supposed to say, break a leg.

EVONNE   Oh . . . that sounds a little violent. Still, break a
                leg then.

                (EVONNE *exits to the main hall, followed by* LINDA
                and BOB, *who wheels off the wash tub.*)

LEONARD   (*to* KATH, *who is still trying to neaten his repair*)
                It's very good stuff is that. It comes in handy for
                all sorts.

WAYNE   (*to* SUE) I could've taken him you know! It's a
                good job Linda managed to hold me back.

SUE   Silly sod!

LEONARD   I even mended the chain on my bike with it once
                . . . it didn't hold though.

KATH   God knows what we're going to do if Helen
                doesn't come back! It's all my fault.

LEONARD   But she's a strange one though, that Helen.

KATH   How perceptive!

LEONARD   Oh, I notice things you know . . . you'd be
            surprised. Take Evonne for example . . . I'd say
            that she was a bit of a nervy type . . . I can usually
            spot them.

            (LEONARD *moves towards the coach.*)

            (*proudly*) What do you think to her then?

KATH   Who?

LEONARD   (*pointing*) I modelled her on the Coronation
            Coach . . . accurate down to the very last detail.

KATH   God save the Queen!

LEONARD   Already? I'd best get her through then.

KATH   It's not on . . . *she's* not on until the second act.

LEONARD   Oh, but I want her ready in the wings for her
            grand entrance.

KATH   We haven't got any wings!

            (LEONARD *moves around to the back of the coach
            and carries it to the door which leads through to
            the main hall. The coach is several inches too
            high to fit through the doorway.* KATH *and* SUE
            watch in disbelief as LEONARD *vainly attempts to
            force the coach through.*)

            Problems?

LEONARD   Just a small technical hitch as we set designers
            like to call it.

SUE   Didn't you measure it!

LEONARD   Well, that's what I'm just having trouble bringing
            myself to terms with. I suspect there's been some
            degree of shrinkage in the door frame since I took
            the critical dimensions. No worry though . . .
            we'll get her through somehow.

(LEONARD *places the coach against the wall and stands back to study the problem as he takes a sandwich out of his back pocket.* KATH *shakes her head and goes over to listen at the entrance to the main hall.*)

KATH   I hope it all goes well for Evonne's sake.

LEONARD   I'm sure it will . . . I have every confidence. Of course I've had a lot of experience performing. I don't know why people get nervous about it. It's just like falling off a log to me.

KATH   Shhh . . . the curtains are opening.

(*Long pause.*)

It seems very quiet . . .

SUE   Well, there's not many in the audience.

KATH   No, on stage . . . who's got the first line?

(SUE *picks up a script.*)

SUE   Er . . . it's the Baron . . . Leonard!

LEONARD   What?

SUE   You're on!

LEONARD   (*panicking*) Am I . . . am I in this bit?

(EVONNE *rushes in frantically from the hall.*)

EVONNE   Leonard!

LEONARD   Yes, I know. I was just having my tea.

(EVONNE *and* LEONARD *get into a tangle as she tries to push him through into the hall and he tries to finish his sandwich.* DAVID *enters from the car park.*)

DAVID   I can't find her . . . she's vanished into thin air!

KATH   Oh no! Come on, Leonard, get on!

LEONARD   Right . . . I'm on my way.

(LEONARD *finally rushes out to the main hall clasping the remains of his sandwich.*)

SUE   What are we going to do!

KATH   There's only one way round it. Evonne . . . you'll have to go on.

EVONNE   (*horrified*) What?

SUE   We'll have to improvise a costume.

(LEONARD *reappears from the hall.*)

LEONARD   What do I say?

KATH   Say anything!

SUE   (*reading*) It's "Hello, Cinders, you're making a super job of darning those socks".

LEONARD   (*after digesting the information for a second*) Right.

(LEONARD *rushes out again as* SUE *grabs hold of a reluctant* EVONNE *to lead her to the changing room.*)

SUE   Come on, Evonne, let's get you ready.

EVONNE   No, I can't! I won't!

SUE   (*firmly*) You'll have to.

(SUE *and* EVONNE *tussle with each other as* LEONARD *reappears, thrusts the remains of his sandwich into* KATH's *hand, and rushes out again.*)

LINDA   (*off, desperately trying to fill in*) Oh, what a nice day. I wonder where my father is . . . the Baron . . . I wonder where he is . . . Father, where are you . . . father . . .

KATH   What a start!

LEONARD   (*off*) Hello jobbers, you're making a darn good
            soup of those sockings.

KATH   (*sadly*) Just like falling off a log.

            (*Curtain Falls.*)

Scene Two

The final night of the pantomime. The curtain opens to find
LEONARD *in the room by himself, setting up his projector.*
Various props are scattered around the room including the
wash tub and the coach which has had the top sawn off it. The
rest of the cast of the pantomime can be heard off stage,
singing the final chorus of "Super Day". When they finish
there is sparse applause. Eventually HELEN *and* BOB *appear*
from the main hall.

HELEN   Super day, super pantomime! I have never been so
            humiliated in all my life as during these past six
            nights.

BOB   I thought it went quite well . . . all things
            considered.

HELEN   But that's the trouble with you, Bob . . . you don't
            consider anything or anybody! All those cheap ad-
            libs at my expense.

BOB   Well, they raised a few laughs . . . people are
            supposed to laugh at panto you know?

HELEN   But not at me!

BOB   Well, if you didn't like it you shouldn't have
            reappeared on the first night should you?

HELEN   You know very well that I only came back to save
            Donal the acute embarrassment of seeing his wife
            make an utter fool of herself. He practically
            begged me.

BOB   (*smiling disarmingly*) Well, I suppose beggars
            can't be choosers!

(BOB *turns away, leaving* HELEN *to puzzle over his comment.* SUE *enters and, seeing* LEONARD *goes to him.*)

SUE   What happened to you! You missed the whole of that last scene . . . and the curtain call.

LEONARD   (*confused*) Did I? I didn't think I was in that bit.

SUE   Of course you were . . . you've been in it for the last five nights, haven't you? (*To* BOB.) I'm sure he hasn't got all his paddles in the water!

BOB   Who?

SUE   Leonard "where am I, what am I doing here" Trotter.

BOB   I thought he was improving . . . he was on stage at the right time twice tonight!

           (KATH, WAYNE, LINDA *and* DAVID *enter.* DAVID *is immediately grabbed by* HELEN *who takes him aside.*)

KATH   Well done, Wayne. You got all your words right tonight . . . even the two syllable ones.

WAYNE   (*modestly*) Yeah . . . I tried to hold everything together. I could see you were all going through a tough patch.

LINDA   What a hero!

WAYNE   I do my best. I'm just going out for some fresh air.

           (WAYNE *goes towards the exit to the car park.*)

LINDA   Do you want a pen?

WAYNE   What?

LINDA   Never mind.

           (WAYNE *exits.*)

	(*to* Kath) He's done that after every performance you know. I followed him last night . . . he goes round to the main door and hangs around waiting for people to ask for his autograph.

KATH   I don't suppose he'll have got writer's cramp!

LINDA   Not exactly. I believe he did manage to force one on to his mum. (*Hesitant.*) Kath . . . I just wanted to say that I'm glad we're talking at last . . . and about you and Bob . . . you know . . . making up. I just got it all wrong. You see, I thought . . .

KATH   (*kindly*) I know. I was probably being over optimistic . . . I sometimes pray for someone to come along and take him off my hands!

             (EVONNE *enters from the main hall. She has a small bottle of gin in her hand which she hurriedly tries to conceal as she remembers it. She has drunk sufficient to calm her nerves!*)

EVONNE   Well done everybody. That was super. I'm so proud of you all.

BOB   (*looking sideways at the bottle*) How many in tonight?

EVONNE   (*excitedly*) Twenty six.

BOB   Sure you weren't seeing double?

EVONNE   What? Oh this? It's just water actually. (*She looks around furtively.*) Is Donal here?

BOB   No, you're quite safe . . . we won't tell him if you don't!

EVONNE   Tell him? . . . Oh, I see what you mean . . . joke . . . super. (*Hurriedly changing the subject.*) Don't you think it's marvellous . . . twenty six!

BOB   Yes, great.

EVONNE   And eleven of them stayed right until the very end!

BOB	Fabulous.
	(LEONARD *wanders over pulling a rather crumpled note out of his pocket.*)
LEONARD	(*to* EVONNE) Your husband, the Vicar as I call him, left this for you. He said he had to get on with his sermon for tomorrow.
EVONNE	Thank you, Leonard. I was rather hoping he'd stay for the party but he's such a busy man. The good work must be done as he says.
BOB	Well, you'll be able to let your hair down if he's not here.
EVONNE	Oh, I don't know about that!
	(EVONNE *takes the note to one side and reads it. Her expression becomes glum.*)
BOB	Right, beer anyone . . . David?
KATH	Come on, Bob. Let's get changed first.
DAVID	There's no harm in making a start.
	(KATH *and* SUE *exit to the changing room.* DAVID *and* BOB *go into the kitchen and open a case of canned beer.*)
HELEN	I wonder if you might pass me a glass of wine, David. Medium white, please.
DAVID	We've only got beer at the moment . . . I'll fetch the rest in from the car in a minute.
HELEN	No, that's alright. A small glass of beer would be quite refreshing.
	(*As* BOB *and* DAVID *leave the kitchen,* BOB *grabs an extra can for* HELEN *which he shakes violently.*)
BOB	(*handing the can to* HELEN) There you go, Sis.

HELEN   But I couldn't possibly drink out of that! . . . it's
            common.

BOB   Sorry . . . glasses are in my car.

            (BOB *and* DAVID *exit to the changing room
            followed by* HELEN. *As she exits she opens the can
            and sprays herself.*)

HELEN   (*shrieking*) You did that on purpose!

LINDA   (*seeing* EVONNE *looking glum*) You alright,
            Evonne?

EVONNE   Yes . . . super. It's just a little disappointing,
            Donal rushing off like that.

LINDA   I'm sure he must be very busy.

EVONNE   Yes . . . no peace for the wicked . . . oh, not that
            Donal's wicked of course, he's a vicar.

LINDA   Pure as the driven snow.

EVONNE   Pardon?

LINDA   Vicars.

EVONNE   Oh yes . . . super.

LINDA   Aren't you going to have a drink?

EVONNE   Well, actually, I'm not sure whether we ought to
            be drinking here really. I don't think Donal would
            approve. Our parties are usually lemonade and
            crisps.

LINDA   (*going to the kitchen*) Come on, you've got to
            have one . . . it's all over, you can celebrate.

EVONNE   Oh, I don't know . . . maybe just a little one then.

LINDA   (*handing a can to* EVONNE) There you are . . .
            cheers.

EVONNE   Oh . . . yes, cheers. (*She takes a small sip.*) Gosh,
              it's quite strong isn't it! I'm not sure whether I
              can manage a whole one . . . especially on top of
              the . . . water I had earlier.

LINDA   Of course you can. It'll do you good.

EVONNE   Yes, I suppose so. Super.

              (EVONNE *goes into the kitchen and starts tidying
              things up.*)

LINDA   Aren't you changing, Leonard?

LEONARD   I just want to finish setting up first. I always like
              to check my equipment for defects . . . just in case
              it's sustained any damage in transit.

LINDA   I'll get you a drink then.

LEONARD   No, not for me. I never drink when I'm doing a
              talk . . . it doesn't pay to drink when you're
              operating heavy machinery. (*He switches on the
              projector which shines onto a screen placed
              against one of the walls.*) This is my test slide . . .
              I always use it . . . it's a nineteen hundred and
              two traction engine, quite a beauty.

LINDA   Yes . . . isn't it! It seems a bit blurred!

LEONARD   Blurred? You must have bad eyes . . . it looks
              perfectly alright to me. (*Switching off the
              projector.*) Righto, that's got it nicely. We seem
              to be fully functional.

LINDA   Come on then, let's get changed.

LEONARD   Right. I'm glad I've got that done. I like to make
              sure everything's ready for action. Pre-flight
              checking as I like to call it.

              (LINDA *and* LEONARD *exit to the changing room as*
              WAYNE *enters from the car park. He sees the
              room empty and* EVONNE *busy in the kitchen. With
              a smirk on his face he takes a slide out of his
              pocket and slips it amongst the slides next to the*

projector. He is about to go into the changing
rooms as EVONNE *comes out of the kitchen.*)

EVONNE   Jolly well done tonight, Wayne.

WAYNE   Thanks. (*He sees the can in her hand.*) You soon
          got stuck in.

EVONNE   Oh, yes it's dreadful isn't it. I feel a bit like a
          lager lout!

WAYNE   You should've seen me and my mates the other
          night . . . absolutely rat ars . . . ratted we were!

EVONNE   Ratted?

WAYNE   Pissed, you know . . . oh, sorry. I'd better get
          changed.

          (WAYNE *is about to exit when he has a change of*
          mind and comes back to EVONNE *hesitantly.*)

          Evonne . . . I wonder if you could give me a piece
          of advice?

EVONNE   Well, I'll try. Not that I'm very good at that sort
          of thing. What would you like to know?

WAYNE   It's just that . . . well, I've got a friend.

EVONNE   Oh, super!

WAYNE   No, I haven't finished yet. You see, this friend . . .
          he fancies this bird . . . girl, right. But the
          trouble is . . . he's not, you know . . . not very
          good at it . . . talking and all that. I mean
          obviously I could put him right, but I thought you
          might have some ideas . . . you know, being a
          sort of a woman.

EVONNE   What kind of ideas?

WAYNE   Well like, how to make conversations and that . . .
          you know, proper ones that people listen to . . .
          sort of intellict . . . inter . . . clever ones.

EVONNE   But why does he want to sound intellectual?

WAYNE   That's it, that's the word! I mean it's better isn't
          it . . . for chatting up birds.

EVONNE   I don't think it matters really. Why can't he just
          be himself?

WAYNE   But he's a complete Wally aren't I . . . aren't he.

EVONNE   Well I'm not really sure that I can help you very
          much. I'm hopeless at talking . . . I never know
          what to say to anybody. I was dreadful with Donal
          . . . I just used to stutter at him. I don't know why
          he married me really. Every morning I wake up
          and look at him and think, why me?

WAYNE   I don't think I could marry a vicar.

EVONNE   Oh, it's super, really it is. I mean there's always
          so much to do . . . organizing things and visiting
          people. It's just a pity that I'm hopeless at it. I
          sometimes visit old people to keep them company
          and we just end up staring at each other. One lady
          said I mustn't go any more because I interrupt her
          television viewing!

WAYNE   (sympathetic) Don't worry . . . I'm sure you'll get
          better.

EVONNE   Oh, yes . . . I suppose so. Donal keeps telling me
          that I've got to stick at it. He says that there's an
          art in getting people to do what they don't want to
          do; you just have to make them feel guilty . . . I'm
          sort of working on that, but the trouble is I end up
          feeling guilty myself. I mean, I don't think
          anybody wanted to do this pantomime really.

WAYNE   I did. I've enjoyed it. I thought you did a really
          good job.

EVONNE   You don't have to say that. I know what I'm like.
          I often think I shouldn't have married Donal . . .
          I'm not right for him . . . he probably wishes he
          hadn't married me.

WAYNE   Don't be stupid! He must have married you
         because he loved you. As long as he loves you the
         other things don't matter.

EVONNE   But perhaps they become more important though,
         as time goes by. Anyway, we shouldn't be talking
         about me. It's your friend that needs the help.

WAYNE   Yeah . . . no! (*Thinking deeply.*) I just sorted it
         out myself. Of course I don't see why he's got
         any problems . . . I mean I've never had any
         trouble pulling the chicks . . . know what I mean?

         (WAYNE *goes to exit to the changing room.*)

         Thanks, Evonne. (*Exits.*)

EVONNE   (*to herself*) What for? (*She looks at the note from
         Donal.*) I'm sorry Donal . . . I've done it again.

         (EVONNE *drinks the rest of her beer in one go and
         then gets another one from the kitchen. She takes
         a long drink from it.* DAVID *enters from the
         changing room. He is casually dressed.*)

DAVID   On your own?

EVONNE   Yes, I seem to have been deserted.

DAVID   (*going to the kitchen and getting two cans*) Here
         you are. Get this down you.

EVONNE   But I've only just . . . Alright then, it is rather
         nice isn't it. (*She takes another big drink.*) Donal
         never drinks beer, although on special occasions
         he sometimes has one of those drinking and
         driving ones.

DAVID   Fun-free lager.

EVONNE   Is it? I thought it was something to do with the
         alcohol content . . . Oh, I see what you mean . . .
         joke . . . super!

         (BOB *and* SUE *enter from the changing room. They
         are casually dressed.*)

BOB   Right, let's get this party going. I'll get the
                glasses out of the car.

DAVID   Would you get the wine as well, Bob. It's in the
                boot.

                (*He throws* BOB *his car keys.* BOB *exits to the car
                park.*)

EVONNE   I hope this won't turn into one of those things you
                read about . . . where everybody throws their car
                keys in and people . . . you know, swop.

DAVID   No chance . . . it's far too dangerous . . . some
                poor innocent might get Helen!

SUE   I suppose Leonard would have to throw his bike
                clips in . . . or his bike. Have you seen it? It must
                be older than he is! And he still insists on locking
                it up . . . the lock's worth more than the bike is!

EVONNE   (*starting to lose her inhibitions*) Gosh, wouldn't it
                be funny if somebody stole the lock and left the
                bike!

                (EVONNE *starts giggling wildly and the others look
                at her in amazement.*)

SUE   Hilarious!

                (*The car alarm sounds from the car park. It
                continues for a few seconds and then stops.*)

                There goes Bob with his party piece . . . he's
                always doing that!

                (DAVID *smiles and then suddenly remembers.*)

DAVID   How often does he do it?

SUE   What?

DAVID   That's where I've seen him! I knew it . . . I knew
                I'd seen him somewhere. A few months ago . . .

he was trying to get into a car. John was with me
in the patrol car . . . we chased him for ages.

SUE   (*not knowing whether to laugh or be anxious*) But
            it was his car. He hadn't done anything wrong.

DAVID   So why did he run off?

SUE   It's a long story . . . I'll tell you later. He lost you
            in Tesco's you know. He spent a fortune.

DAVID   That's where he went! We couldn't figure it out.

SUE   (*concerned*) You're not going to do anything are
            you?

DAVID   I don't know . . . no, not if it was his car. I do
            think a little retribution's called for though . . .
            we were knackered!

SUE   Oh, David!

           (BOB *staggers in with a box of glasses and two
           wine boxes. He takes them over to the kitchen
           counter.* DAVID *winks at* SUE.)

DAVID   Forget your alarm?

BOB   Yes, I'm always doing that.

DAVID   Really?

BOB   (*remembering that* DAVID *is a policeman*) What?
            Oh no . . . I say always but I mean hardly ever . . .
            in fact, I think that's the first time it's happened.
            It's Kath . . . she tends to forget it. (*Forcing a
            laugh.*) Women, eh!

DAVID   Yeah. Actually it reminds me of a few months
            ago. I was on patrol with John, my mate, and we
            saw a bloke trying to break into a car. We chased
            him all over the place but we never got him.

BOB   (*nervous*) What a pity . . . I don't suppose you got
            a good look at him did you . . . if he was running
            away.

DAVID	I only caught a glimpse, but John swears he'd know him anywhere!
BOB	Still . . . it was a long time ago.
DAVID	Oh, John never forgets a face. He was here last night actually . . . to see the panto.
BOB	What!
DAVID	In fact he said afterwards that he wants to see you again.

(DAVID *smiles at* BOB *who doesn't know how to take it*.)

BOB	(*weakly*) I'll sort the drinks out.

(BOB *goes into the kitchen to unpack the glasses*.)

EVONNE	Super party isn't it.
SUE	I think you ought to go slowly with that, Evonne. You're not used to it.
EVONNE	Oh, it's alright. I'm quite getting the hang of it. (*She takes another large gulp*.) Was that some wine I saw Bob bringing in?
SUE	Take my advice. Don't mix them. You'll get a hangover.
EVONNE	Oh, I mustn't have a hangover. It's Sunday tomorrow . . . Donal's big day . . . he gets to do his sermon.
DAVID	Well, if you carry on at this rate, you'll be sleeping through it!
EVONNE	Oh, I can't do that . . . I'm usually the only one who stays awake! (*Giggling*.) Everybody else snores terribly!
SUE	(*to* DAVID) I don't think she should have any more.
EVONNE	Actually I have a confession to make . . . sometimes I do fall asleep . . . isn't that awful! I try not to . . . but I do.

SUE   (*teasing*) Evonne, that's dreadful!

EVONNE   (*giggling*) Yes, isn't it. I think maybe I ought to
               tell Donal, but I daren't.

SUE   I shouldn't if I were you. Just snooze quietly to
               yourself.

EVONNE   No, not about that, silly . . . not about falling
               asleep. I mean about his sermons . . . they're
               terrible . . . they're so boring!

SUE   Surely not!

EVONNE   They are . . . dreadfully dull. I often think I could
               do much better. (*Giggling even louder.*) Isn't that
               horrid of me!

               (BOB, *unable to contain his fears any longer,
               approaches* DAVID.)

BOB   David?

DAVID   Yeah?

BOB   (*fearfully*) You know you said that this . . . John,
               wanted to see me again. What about?

DAVID   What? . . . no, not personally. He wanted to see
               you again on the stage . . . he thought you were
               very good.

BOB   (*relieved*) That's all!

DAVID   (*enjoying himself*) Yes. Why, was there something
               else?

BOB   No absolutely not.

DAVID   Fine. (*Casually.*) Do you go in Tesco's at all?

BOB   (*alarmed again*) Tesco!

DAVID   The supermarket . . . you know.

BOB   Er, no . . . well yes . . . no.

DAVID	I got the wine there. They do quite a good range if you've got time to browse.
BOB	Ah well, I haven't you see . . . I wouldn't.
DAVID	You ought to dodge in there sometime and have a look.
BOB	(*uncertain*) Yes.
DAVID	(*unable to keep it up any longer*) Don't worry, Bob . . . John didn't recognize you. You had all that make up on. Don't run away next time though. We might catch you!

(DAVID *turns away, leaving* BOB *feeling rather sheepish.* KATH *enters from the changing room. She is dressed smartly but informally.*)

KATH	Drink, Bob.

(BOB *goes back to the kitchen to pour some wine.*)

DAVID	You're looking good, Kath.
KATH	Thank you, David. I feel a bit under-dressed compared with Helen though . . . wait 'til you see her!
DAVID	Not her Brownie uniform is it?
SUE	David quite fancies ladies in uniform don't you?
DAVID	Yes, well . . . (*Imitating* HELEN.) We people in the uniformed services must stick together.

(EVONNE *starts giggling insanely. They all look at her.*)

EVONNE	That sounded just like silly old Helen!
KATH	I think you ought to sit down, Evonne.
EVONNE	No, I'm fine. I'm super, really. (*She takes a large gulp of beer.*)
KATH	Slow down . . . it's not lemonade, you know.

EVONNE   No this is far nicer. Boring old Donal doesn't
               know what he's missing!

               (BOB *exits from the kitchen and is about to give*
               KATH *her glass of wine when* EVONNE *takes it from*
               him.)

               Thank you . . . super.

               (BOB *shrugs his shoulders and goes back towards*
               the kitchen. HELEN *enters from the changing room.*
               She is wearing what she considers to be a trendy
               dress, complete with shoulder pads, etc.)

BOB   (*whistling*) And here she is, this evening's special
               guest. A big round of applause for . . .
               (*Confidentially, to* HELEN.) Sorry, is it Joan
               Collins or Phil?

HELEN   I hope that you are not going to continue like this
               all evening, Bob.

BOB   Would I do that, Helen! Look, as a gesture of
               good will, I'll even get you a drink . . . or do you
               want to change first?

HELEN   (*icily*) Wine please, Bob.

EVONNE   (*giggling*) She's not wearing her Brownies . . .
               you said she was wearing her Brownies!
               (*Imitating* HELEN.) We uniforms must stick
               together.

HELEN   (*horrified*) Is she drunk!

EVONNE   (*imitating her*) Is she drunk.

HELEN   It's disgusting. Just you wait until I see Donal!

EVONNE   Knock knock.

KATH   (*trying to calm* EVONNE *down*) Not now, Evonne.

EVONNE   No, come on . . . knock knock.

KATH   (*reluctantly*) Who's there?

EVONNE   Donal.

KATH   Donal who?

EVONNE   Donal Duckworth!

            (*This sends* EVONNE *into paroxysms of laughter,
            whilst everybody else looks on in amazement.* BOB
            returns from the kitchen and gives drinks to KATH
            and HELEN.)

KATH   No more for Evonne, right!

            (LINDA, WAYNE *and* LEONARD *enter from the
            changing room. They are casually dressed, with*
            LEONARD *looking as scruffy as ever.*)

LEONARD   Is everybody ready for the slide show? I'd like to
            get on because time's pressing, so if you'll just
            assemble yourselves.

KATH   Just a minute, Leonard, before you start. We've
            got something to do first. Bob?

BOB   Oh, yeah . . . right.

            (BOB *races into the changing room.*)

KATH   Evonne, would you like to come over here a
            minute?

            (EVONNE *goes to* KATH *looking rather baffled.*)

            We just wanted to say thank you, Evonne . . . and
            very well done. We think you put a lot of effort in
            and it wouldn't have worked without you . . .

            (BOB *returns with a bouquet of flowers, which he
            passes to* KATH. *She gives them to* EVONNE.)

            We all got together . . . (*Glowering at* HELEN.) . . .
            most of us got together to give you these. Well
            done.

            (*They all applaud and whistle, with the exception
            of* HELEN.)

EVONNE   Gosh, I didn't expect this . . . they're . . .

ALL   Super.

EVONNE   Yes . . . super.

BOB   Speech . . . speech . . .

              (*This call is picked up by the others.*)

EVONNE   Well, I was going to say a few words later, but
              I'll do it now if you like. (*She produces a piece of
              paper.*) Donal wrote it for me so it's probably
              ever so boring!

HELEN   I can not believe what I'm hearing!

KATH   Sssh!

HELEN   Don't you 'Sssh' me!

EVONNE   (*reading*) Dear friends, we are gathered here
              today to celebrate the fulfilment of a vision. This
              vision was to bring the gift of joy and laughter to
              the people of our parish, through the medium of
              pantomime, and we give thanks for the
              completion of this noble endeavour . . . I told you
              it was boring . . . I feel certain that our audiences
              have left the hall with uplifted spirits, having
              shared in this great adventure. As you know, the
              proceeds are to be used to swell our church bell
              appeal and we look forward to the day when our
              bells will be a-pealing . . . I think that bit was
              supposed to be funny. I thank you for your efforts
              in this most worthy cause. May the Lord bless you
              and keep you, signed the Reverend Donal
              Duckworth.

              (*They all applaud politely, including* HELEN.)

HELEN   He has such a way with words. Of course, she
              read it very badly!

EVONNE   I thought it was boring.

BOB   So come on, Evonne . . . don't keep us in
              suspenders . . . how much did we raise?

SUE   Yeah . . . come on . . . how much?

EVONNE   (*reluctantly*) Well, Donal did leave me a little
            note tonight. Apparently, over the six nights we
            took . . . (*She produces the note that* LEONARD
            gave her earlier.) . . . one hundred and thirty five
            pounds, fifty pence.

ALL   Well done, great, etc.

SUE   So, all that goes towards Donal's bells?

EVONNE   Well, I'm afraid not . . . Donal's made a note of
            the hire charge for the hall so the final total's a
            bit less.

KATH   What? But we were doing it for the church!
            Surely we don't have to pay for the hall!

LEONARD   I think you'll find that we'll have to pay a charge
            because there'll be things that have to be covered,
            such as your heating and your lighting and your
            cleaning and your toilet rolls and . . .

KATH   (*gently*) Leonard . . . shut up, there's a dear.

LEONARD   Oh . . . right.

KATH   So what's the final figure, Evonne?

EVONNE   (*miserably*) Forty two pounds fifty.

KATH   Oh! Well that's not bad. At least it's a profit.

EVONNE   No it isn't . . . that's what we owe Donal the hire
            charge is bigger than our takings.

KATH   What!

BOB   Just hold on a minute . . . you mean we have to
            pay Donal for the privilege of trying to make
            some money for him?

EVONNE   Oh I don't think he'll make us pay it. He'll get
            round it somehow. I'm sorry, it's all my fault.

HELEN   (*gloating*) So, we made a loss did we? Well, I
             predicted right from the start that this would
             happen. Of course, if Donal had seen fit to put me
             in charge, then the end result would have been
             very different. I warned you!

BOB   Do you know something, Helen? You're a
             miserable rat bag!

HELEN   Don't you dare speak to me like that!

SUE   Let's not fall out again! It doesn't matter what the
             end result is. You did a great job, Evonne, and I
             enjoyed doing it . . . we all did.

HELEN   I most certainly didn't!

DAVID   Three cheers for Evonne.

             (DAVID *leads them all in three cheers.* HELEN *does
             not join in.*)

HELEN   I've never seen such a display of mass hysteria in
             all my life.

LEONARD   Can I get on now?

DAVID   Just a moment, Leonard. I've got an
             announcement to make. (*He takes hold of* SUE'S
             hand.) One or two of you might have noticed that
             Sue and I have developed quite a friendship over
             the last couple of months. Well actually, it goes a
             bit further than that. Earlier on this week I asked
             Sue to marry me and well, I don't know why, but
             she said yes.

             (*They all cheer with the exception of* HELEN *who
             looks stunned.*)

             We wanted you to be the first to know because it
             was all this that brought us together.

             (*Everybody talks excitedly with the exception of*
             HELEN, *who sits quietly on her own.* LEONARD
             moves over to HELEN.)

LEONARD   I knew something was going on there . . . I told
            you. (*To everybody.*) I wonder if I might get on
            now . . . I've a packed itinerary.

            (KATH *glances sharply at* BOB, *who takes the hint.*)

BOB   Ah Leonard.

LEONARD   I'm sure you'll all find it most invigorating. In
            fact I believe I'm correct in saying that this may
            be one of my finest productions yet. I've left no
            stone unturned in my research.

BOB   It's just that we thought . . . with time being
            limited . . . it may be best to curtail the talk.

LEONARD   Oh, there are no worries there. I was very aware
            of the time factor during my preparation. Window
            of opportunity as I call it. I set myself very strict
            limitations on the length and so forth.

BOB   (*uncertain*) Good. How long?

LEONARD   Just under ninety minutes.

KATH   What!

EVONNE   Sounds like one of Donal's sermons.

LEONARD   Of course, if I take it at pace I can probably knock
            five minutes off that. Whenever you're ready.

KATH   (*sharply*) Bob!

BOB   It's just that . . . (*Glancing around for support.*) .
            . . by curtail, what I actually meant . . . well *we*,
            what *we* meant is more kind of . . . abandon.

KATH   Cancel.

            (LEONARD *looks totally stunned.*)

DAVID   (*helpfully*) Or postpone, 'til another day.

LEONARD   But I'm all geared up.

KATH   But so are we, Leonard . . . for a party. We want
            to dance and . . . you know.

EVONNE   (*giggling*) Throw car keys in. But *you* can't 'cos
            you've only got a silly old bike.

HELEN   Would someone please control that woman. I shall
            be having words with Donal about her behaviour
            this evening.

            (EVONNE *blows a loud raspberry at* HELEN *who is
            dumb-struck.* DAVID *rushes to intervene before an
            argument develops.*)

DAVID   So, that's settled then. Alright, Leonard?

LEONARD   But I'm all set up.

KATH   But we don't want to . . .

BOB   (*stepping in quickly*) Look . . . let's compromise,
            we'll do both. Leonard can give his talk while we
            all mingle. Ok? Great. Off you go, Leonard don't
            mind us. Let's get some background music on.

            (BOB *switches on the cassette deck, then moves
            behind the counter to act as barman.* DAVID *and*
            SUE *move to a quiet corner to "smooch". The rest
            fall into a party atmosphere. The only exceptions
            are* LEONARD, *who stands by his projector not
            knowing how to handle the situation, and* HELEN,
            who sits quietly by herself.)

WAYNE   Okay, let's party.

            (WAYNE *"whoops" wildly and starts to dance
            around extravagantly.*)

            Come on, Evonne . . . get down and boogie!

            (KATH *sees* EVONNE *looking rather uncertain and
            leads her down so that they both dance with*
            WAYNE. LINDA, *seeing* HELEN *alone, goes over to
            her.*)

LINDA   Don't you think it's great about David and Sue?

HELEN	Obviously I misjudged him. I thought he had more sense. He and Susan aren't well suited . . . far from it. It'll all end in tears, believe you me. But if David expects me to be there to help him pick up the pieces, then he'll be sadly disappointed.
LINDA	But they're happy. Come on, join in.
HELEN	No thank you. *I*, at least can retain *my* dignity.

(LINDA *shrugs and goes to join in the dancing.* LEONARD, *who has been watching events in dismay, decides to press on regardless.*)

LEONARD	Are you all settled then?
BOB	We can't wait, Leonard.
LEONARD	Right, then I'll begin. (*He starts reading from a large wad of handwritten notes. He is generally ignored apart from occasional glances and comments.*) It was first introduced into Britain at Drury Lane Theatre in seventeen hundred and two by a man called . . . hang on, this is page three. I won't be a moment, I'm just out of order.

(LEONARD *shuffles through his papers.*)

BOB	We don't mind if you miss the odd sheet out, Leonard.
LEONARD	No, I'll get it right. I don't want to disappoint you . . . right, here we are . . . Ladies and Gentlemen, welcome to my little talk on the history of pantomime. (*He starts reading his notes again.*) Now, you probably don't know this, but the word pantomime comes from the word pantomimus, which means imitator of all things. It first became very popular in Rome during the reign of the Emperor August . . . us. Twenty seven BC to AD fourteen. After this period, during which it flourished, it gradually became less popular and for many . . .
BOB	They probably had better things to do!

LEONARD   Pardon?

BOB   I was just saying . . . they probably had better
            things to do . . . like throwing Christians to the
            lions!

LEONARD   Oh, right . . . yes. Now following this period . . .

BOB   That's probably where the expression "it's behind
            you" comes from.

LEONARD   (*exasperated*) I'm sorry but I'm not used to being
            tampered with when I'm giving a talk. Now, can I
            get on?

SUE   Couldn't we have a few slides first . . . just to get
            us in the mood?

LEONARD   Well, I don't know . . . that's not how I'd planned
            it, I'd be losing my sequence.

            (LEONARD *is flustered and starts fiddling through
            his papers and his slides.* WAYNE *leans over to*
            LINDA *as they continue to dance.*)

WAYNE   This should be good! I've spiced it up a bit. Just
            wait 'til it comes up!

LINDA   (*suspicious*) What have you done, Wayne?

WAYNE   (*sniggering*) You know those photos that you took
            at the conference?

LINDA   Which ones?

WAYNE   At the conference party, where Bob's playing that
            game with all those women.

LINDA   Where his trousers are round his ankles!

WAYNE   I got a slide made . . . it's mixed up with that lot!

LINDA   (*horrified*) You idiot!

WAYNE   It's only a bit of a laugh. It'll liven things up!

LINDA   And what about Kath . . . is she going to see the
            funny side of it?

WAYNE   But it was only a party game . . . she'll understand
            won't she?

LINDA   Do you want to risk it?

WAYNE   I'll go and get it back.

LINDA   You can't now . . . you'll just draw attention to it!
            I'll warn Bob.

            (LINDA *moves over to* BOB. EVONNE *has been
            trying to copy* WAYNE's *dancing style and is now
            almost as bad as him.*)

EVONNE   (*to* KATH) This boogeling about is rather good fun
            isn't it. I'm looking forward to Leonard's slides.

KATH   If he ever manages to get round to them! Come
            on, Leonard, do something.

LEONARD   But you've got me out of sequence now! I'm all
            disjointed. I don't know whether you want slides
            or a talk. I had a good bit coming up next.

BOB   (*chanting*) We want the slides . . . we want the
            slides.

LINDA   (*to* BOB) You don't want the slides!

BOB   Yes I do.

LINDA   Take it from me, you don't.

            (LINDA *whispers into* BOB's *ear. He is horrified.*)

BOB   (*chanting louder*) We want the talk . . . we want
            the talk.

LEONARD   Right, I'll start off by showing you the slides I
            took on the first night.

HELEN   (*who has decided that* LEONARD *is her last hope*)
            Is there anything I can do to assist, Leonard?

(HELEN *moves over to* LEONARD *at the projector and starts reorganising everything.*)

LEONARD   No, it's alright, I'm just getting sorted.

KATH   (*singing*) Why are we waiting, why are we waiting
            . . .

HELEN   Be quiet, Katherine. We're doing our best aren't
            we Lenny.

KATH   Oh, it's "Lenny" now is it? When did you become
            interested in slide shows, Helen?

HELEN   Take no notice of her, Lenny. As it happens,
            Leonard and I share many common interests.

LEONARD   You're getting me all out of order.

HELEN   It doesn't matter, Lenny this one will do.

LEONARD   But it won't match my script.

HELEN   (*impatiently*) It doesn't matter.

            (HELEN *switches the projector on and they all look
            at the screen.* BOB *heaves a sigh of relief when he
            sees the subject.*)

KATH   I can't make it out!

DAVID   Could you focus it up a bit, Leonard.

LEONARD   There's nothing wrong with that . . . it's crystal
            clear.

EVONNE   (*squinting and then squealing excitedly*) I think
            it's me . . . look, I'm sure it is.

HELEN   Move on, Lenny, we don't want that one.

            (HELEN *takes the slide out of the projector.*)

BOB   (*hopefully*) Thanks, Leonard, that was great . . . I
            haven't enjoyed myself so much for years. Do you
            want a hand packing up?

LEONARD   But I've only just got myself started!

BOB   But it was good . . . you should always finish
           while you're on top.

HELEN   Take no notice, Lenny. Carry on.

BOB   But it's Linda . . . she feels sick don't you?

LINDA   (*slow on the uptake*) Do I?

EVONNE   Actually, I think I do as well.

           (*Several more slides are shown in quick
           succession, each of them badly focused, although
           it is just possible to make out the various
           characters in a range of poses. They all quickly
           become bored and begin to dance more and
           largely ignore the slides.* BOB *turns the music up
           louder in an attempt to distract them from the
           slides further.* LEONARD *and* HELEN *become
           involved in a minor tussle as she tries to take
           charge of the slide show. The final slide to be
           shown is of* LINDA *changing. She is scantily
           dressed and just behind her is the obscurred
           figure of a man. His hands, though, can be clearly
           seen wrapped around the front of* LINDA *and are
           compromisingly placed.* WAYNE *and* BOB *are the
           first to notice the slide and stop dead, staring
           open-mouthed. Gradually the rest of them see the
           slide and stop dancing.* LINDA *is the last to notice
           as* BOB *stops the music.*)

LINDA   (*indignant*) I didn't know you'd taken that!

LEONARD   I didn't realize that I had!

WAYNE   That quick change into the ball gown always was
           spectacular.

LINDA   Don't be disgusting!

HELEN   (*prudishly*) I agree . . . it's disgusting. Next one,
           Lenny.

EVONNE   (*squinting even harder*) Wait a minute . . . who's
           that helping you change?

LINDA   I don't know . . . I was always in such a rush!

WAYNE   I'd have helped you if you'd asked.

EVONNE   I know who it is!

             (EVONNE *rushes to the screen in horror, to inspect it more closely.*)

KATH   It's too blurred, Evonne.

EVONNE   It's Donal! Look, I think that's his bald patch.

KATH   I don't think so, Evonne. It's not clear enough.

EVONNE   It's Donal. Why was he helping you change . . . he didn't tell me he'd helped you change!

KATH   (*trying to calm her*) But even if it is Donal, he was only helping.

EVONNE   (*distraught*) But he didn't have to put his hand there did he! (*Squinting.*) And there! (*They all squint even harder.*)

KATH   It's just a trick of the camera lens.

LEONARD   Oh no . . . the camera never lies.

EVONNE   (*hysterical*) Take it off . . . stop looking at it!

HELEN   (*gloating*) Well, I think we should leave it up there. It doesn't surprise me that Donal should start to look elsewhere.

LINDA   (*defending herself and* EVONNE) I was only changing!

HELEN   (*knowingly*) Oh, well, that may be how it started, but it's quite obvious how it developed!

EVONNE   (*sobbing*) Take it off . . . stop staring at it.

HELEN   I will not take it off . . . I find it very amusing.

EVONNE   (*in an anguished shout*) Why do you hate me!

(EVONNE *is overcome with emotion and doesn't know what to do. She runs over to the projector and grabs the offending slide together with a handful of other slides. Looking around, she notices the wash tub and runs to it. She stands for a second, looking at the slides and the wash tub and then hurls the slides violently into the water in the tub.* HELEN *moves quickly to her.*)

HELEN   How dare you! Those are Lenny's. (*Turning to the others.*) The woman's obviously deranged . . . completely unhinged. You're all witnesses.

(HELEN *turns back and leans to look into the tub.*)

It's no less than malicious vandalism.

EVONNE   (*shouting*) Shut up.

HELEN   I most certainly will not.

(EVONNE, *on a sudden impulse, suddenly pushes* HELEN'S *head down into the water. She releases her and* HELEN *stands, spluttering, stunned and soaked. There is a long pause as they all look at* HELEN, *waiting for her reaction, but she just stands there in shocked disbelief.* LEONARD *finally breaks the silence.*)

LEONARD   You didn't happen to locate any of my slides while you were in there?

(*For a second* HELEN *looks as though she is about to explode but, deciding to retain what little dignity remains to her, she simply spins on her heels and strides into the changing room.* EVONNE, *realizing what she has just done, bursts into tears.*)

EVONNE   I'm going home!

BOB   Wait a minute, Evonne.

EVONNE   (*shouting as she moves to the exit*) I'm going home.

BOB   It wasn't Donal!

EVONNE   Yes it was.

BOB   No it wasn't . . . it was me.

             (BOB *glances over at* KATH, *who scowls back*.)

KATH   (*angrily*) What did you say!

BOB   I said it was me.

EVONNE   Not . . . not Donal? (*Pause*.) But I thought . . . I
             was sure . . . aren't I silly? (*Suddenly realizing*.)
             Leonard . . . your slides! Helen! I pushed Helen
             into . . . (*Starting to giggle*.) I put Helen in there!

             (*They all try to keep a straight face but one by
             one they start laughing*.)

SUE   Well looks as though that's the end of the show.

LEONARD   Oh no, don't worry, I can press on. There's still
             plenty of slides left.

WAYNE   (*making a decision*) A man's gotta do what a
             man's gotta do!

             (WAYNE *moves to the projector and picks up a
             large box of the remaining slides*.)

             Sorry, Leonard.

             (WAYNE *walks away, picking out slides in turn,
             glancing at them then discarding them over his
             shoulder*.)

LEONARD   Those are my slides . . . what are you doing?

LINDA   The first sensible thing he's done for ages.

LEONARD   (*in a panic*) My slides!

             (LEONARD *chases after* WAYNE *and is torn between
             trying to stop him and picking up the discarded*

slides. He decides on the latter and follows
behind Wayne, *picking up slides and cramming*
them into his pockets.)

There are some good ones in there!

BOB   That's what we're afraid of!

(Linda *starts to help* Leonard *and they both*
follow the trail of slides as Wayne *exits, leading*
them into the car park.)

LINDA   (*as she exits*) You don't have to throw them
              everywhere, Wayne!

SUE   What's all that about?

BOB   (*innocently*) Search me.

DAVID   (*reluctantly*) Come on, Sue. We'd better see if
              Helen's alright.

SUE   Do we have to?

DAVID   It's a hell of a job but someone's got to do it. We
              uniforms et cetera!

EVONNE   (*torn between giggling and feeling guilty*) I think
              I'd better apologise.

(Evonne, Sue *and* David *exit to the changing*
room. Evonne *is staggering rather uncertainly.*
Kath *and* Bob *remain.* Kath *is almost in tears.*
Bob *moves over to her and tries to put his arm*
around her.)

KATH   Keep away from me.

BOB   Kath, come on!

KATH   I trusted you and what happens . . . as soon as my
              back's turned!

BOB   Nothing happened.

KATH   So, what about you and Linda . . . that's nothing
         is it?

BOB   Where were you when Linda had to do that quick
         change?

KATH   On stage . . . out of the way!

BOB   And who were you talking to on stage?

KATH   What's that got do with anything? (*Suddenly
         realizing.*) You . . . I was talking to you!

BOB   Exactly. Let's just hope Evonne doesn't realize
         that.

KATH   But why did you tell Evonne . . . ?

BOB   I had to . . . we couldn't let her go off thinking it
         was Donal could we?

KATH   So, who was it?

         (*There is suddenly a loud shriek from* HELEN, *off,
         in the changing room. It is followed by the sound
         of heated shouting and argument.*)

         (*wearily*) Oh no, not again!

         (WAYNE *enters from the car park. He is down to
         the last few slides. He is still followed by* LEONARD
         and LINDA. LEONARD'S *pockets are now bulging
         and overflowing with slides and he has a huge
         pile cupped in his hands.* WAYNE *discards several
         more slides as he enters, then finally looks at one
         more closely.*)

WAYNE   (*shouting triumphantly*) Yes!

         (WAYNE *waves the slide over his head as a scream
         is suddenly heard from* EVONNE, *off, in the
         changing room. They all glance around with the
         exception of* LEONARD, *who is trying to pick up the
         last few slides, and* BOB, *who takes the
         opportunity to snatch the slide off* WAYNE. KATH

spots his action out of the corner of her eye.
EVONNE *suddenly rushes out of the changing room
in a panic and canons into* LEONARD, *who drops
all the slides again.* EVONNE *looks around, eyes
bulging in terror, then darts away, out through
the kitchen.* KATH, *seeing that* BOB *is momentarily
distracted, snatches the slide off him. She is about
to look at it as* HELEN *storms out of the dressing
room.* HELEN *is bedraggled with a towel wrapped
around her head and she is carrying a "prop"
broomstick threateningly.* DAVID *and* SUE *follow*
HELEN *but pause in the doorway.*)

HELEN   (*deranged with anger*) Where is she!

LINDA   (*innocently*) Who?

                 (HELEN *stalks around the room as* KATH *tries to
                 have a quick look at the slide.* LEONARD, *next to*
                 KATH, *has just about given up on the pile of slides
                 on the floor and looks almost angry. He sees the
                 slide in* KATH'S *hand and snatches it from her.*
                 HELEN *is about to trample through the pile of
                 slides on the floor, but* LEONARD *stops her,
                 holding up his hand in which he is grasping the
                 slide.*)

LEONARD   Careful . . . those are my slides.

                 (HELEN *in a complete fury, looks at* LEONARD,
                 *grabs the slide from his hand and hurls it into the
                 wash tub which is nearby. There is complete
                 silence for several seconds.*)

KATH   (*accusingly to* BOB) What was on that!

BOB   (*innocently*) That? I don't know. Anyway, it was
                 probably out of focus.

                 (*The curtain falls.*)

OUT OF FOCUS

Super Day

Words & Music by
Peter Gordon

VERSE

1. When you're at the pan - to - mime a hap - py end - ing's brill But things would have turned

out much worse with - out the fair - ies' skill Now Cin - der - el - la's got her prince Her

sis - ters end with nil And pus - sy's got his bowl of milk So he can drink his fill.

Cin - ders' friend and in the end wish Cin - ders could be mine. And
Cin - ders' cat and of - ten sat while Cin - ders darned her clothes. And

I'm a sis - ter dev - ious twis - ter Though I look di - vine She's
I'm Prince Charm - ing it's a - larm - ing just how quick love grows I'll

D.%. al Coda

off her nut her beer gut is twice as big as mine.
be his wife and pledge my life to fol - low where he goes.

CODA

rit.

so we say fare - well to this most su - per pan - to - mime.

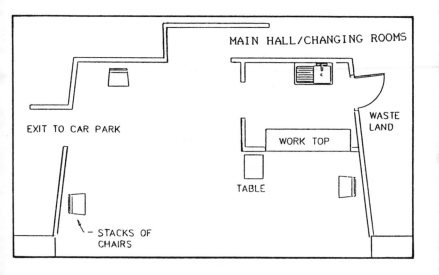

SETTING

The setting may be as complex or simple as desired. In its simplest form there must be clearly marked exits, stacks of chairs and a table. A worktop which is slightly partitioned from the rest of the room would suffice for the kitchen area.

FURNITURE AND PROPERTY LIST

ACT ONE

Scene One

On Stage: Chairs stacked together
            Table
            Coats scattered on floor
            Cardboard boxes containing cans and blankets
            Kettle
            Crockery
            Spoons
            Saucepan
            Jar of Coffee

```
                    Sugar
                    Powdered milk
                    Tray

Off Stage:     Sports bag with badminton racquet (SUE)
               Shopping bag with scripts (EVONNE)
               Sports bag with badminton racquet concealed (BOB)
               Sports bag (BOB)
               Suitcase containing slides and list (LEONARD)
               Slide projector (LEONARD)
               Sports bag containing table tennis bat (DAVID)
               Towel (BOB)
               Rope and handkerchief (WAYNE)

Personal:      Watch (SUE)
               Car keys (KATH)
               Crumpled note (LEONARD)
               Personal stereo (WAYNE)
```

                                Scene Two

```
Strike:        Shopping bag
               Sports bags
               Suitcase
               Cardboard boxes
               Slides
               Projector
               Used crockery

Set:           Re-position furniture
               Cassette player with taped music of "Super Day"
               Painted flat of stove and saucepan
               Coronation coach-shaped flat with cut-out window
               Tray of cups in kitchen area

Personal:      Scripts (ALL)
               Costume, needle and thread (SUE)
               Paint pots, brushes (DAVID and LEONARD)
               Sandwiches (LEONARD)
               Small change (WAYNE)
               Two pound coins (DAVID)
               Two pound coins (BOB)
               Five pound note (SUE)
               Wand (KATH)
```

ACT TWO

Scene One

Strike: Cassette player
Used crockery
Sandwiches
Scripts

Set: Re-position furniture
Wash tub
Dust sheet (on coach flat)

Off Stage: Suitcase containing camera, sandwiches and
insulating tape (LEONARD)

Personal: Wand (KATH)
Script (BOB)

Scene Two

Strike: Camera
Sandwiches
Suitcase
Script

Set: Re-position furniture
Wash tub
Coach flat
Cans of beer
Suitcase containing slides and notes
Projector and screen
Cassette player

Off Stage: Gin bottle (EVONNE)
Box of glasses, two wine boxes (BOB)
Bouquet of flowers (BOB)

Personal: Crumpled note (LEONARD)
Slide (WAYNE)
Car keys (DAVID)
Hand-written speech (EVONNE)

LIGHTING PLOT

ACT ONE

Interior: Artificial lighting
Exterior: Dusk

ACT TWO

Interior: Artificial lighting
Exterior: Dark

EFFECTS PLOT

ACT ONE

Scene One

Cue 1:   KATH ". . . baked beans, burgers and broccoli!"
            Car alarm starts   (page 7)

Cue 2:   KATH ". . . there be a policeman around."
            Car alarm stops   (page 7)

Cue 3:   DAVID "None of my lot here yet?
            Car alarm starts   (page 23)

Cue 4:   SUE ". . . This is one of our opponents."
            Car alarm stops   (page 24)

ACT TWO

Scene Two

Cue 5:   SUE "Hilarious."
            Car alarm sounds briefly then stops   (page 99)